Information Gr

Information Graphics

Bryan Purves BEd (Hons) MCCEd (Hons) FEIDCT

Head of Craft, Design and Technology
The Towers School, Kennington, Kent

Stanley Thornes (Publishers) Ltd

First published in 1987 by:
Stanley Thornes (Publishers) Ltd
Old Station Drive
Leckhampton
CHELTENHAM GL53 0DN
England

British Library Cataloguing in Publication Data

Purves, Bryan
    Information graphics.
    1.   Visual communication.
    I.   Title
    001.56   P93.5

    ISBN 0-85950-674-6

Typeset by Tech-Set, Gateshead, Tyne & Wear.
Printed and bound in Hong Kong by Wing King Tong Ltd.

Contents

Preface

The material in this book is intended to give teachers and students ready access to current thinking on the broadening scope of graphic communication, and an insight into the use of charts, symbols and systems, now becoming commonplace in 16+ examinations in design-related subjects – for example, the AEB Basic Test, GCSE Graphic Communication and GCSE CDT: Design and Communication.

Graphic communication is the means to an end and not an end in itself. We only have to look around in everyday life to see the vast range of signs that are in use whose main objective is to convey a message. It is therefore of the utmost importance that students are given the opportunity to understand and appreciate this form of communication. This book's aim is to develop the ability to understand and communicate information by graphical means in the form of charts, signs and symbols.

Information graphics is a single subject – a way of representing visual images to convey a message. Although in many cases these images are later developed on other surfaces, they are generally on paper during the initial stages. This book provides a unified treatment of the subject, divided into six sections. The first deals with data representation through the use of diagrams, while the second deals with the plotting of land formations and how relevant information is made readily available to the public. Section 3 is concerned with plans of our living environment and domestic services, and leads on to the fourth section which deals specifically with the symbols that are encountered within the home and on household packaging. The fifth section is concerned with the law and signs, and with the different signs that signify specific types of legally required or useful information. Finally, Section 6 provides for practical work in the subject with a small amount of development drawing, giving scope for individuals to use symbols as seems best for particular purposes.

Bryan Purves, 1987

Acknowledgements

The author and publishers express their thanks to the following for permission to reproduce illustrations and for information:

Article Numbering Association (UK) Ltd, pp. 32–5;

Associated Examining Board (AEB), p. 7;

Austin Rover, p. 19;

Autocar, p. 17;

Extracts from British Standards are reproduced by permission of the British Standards Institution, pp. 73, 76–8, 80, 96–8, 113. Complete copies can be obtained from BSI at Linford Wood, Milton Keynes, MK14 6LE;

Caution Magazine/Hi-Lite Signs, pp. 120–7, 129–30;

Department of Transport, p. 131;

Focal Chemical Co., p. 127;

Reproduced with the permission of Her Majesty's Stationery Office, Crown Copyright Reserved, pp. 53–5, 58, 59–65, 68, 128;

Home Laundering Consultative Council, pp. 110–11;

London Regional Examinations Board (LREB), p. 50;

Open University, PET271 *Technology for Teachers*, © 1975 The Open University Press, p. 16, Fig. 1.24;

University of Oxford Delegacy of Local Examinations (OLE), p. 16;

Wallcovering Manufacturer's Association European Federation IGI, p. 112.

The author would like to record his grateful thanks to Stanley Thornes (Publishers) Ltd for their invaluable support and encouragement throughout the preparation of this book.

Egyptian hieroglyphic – a rolled drawing is unrolled, placed on a
drawing board, and the draughtsman commences work.

Section 1

Data Representation

Data can be represented in numerous ways. One form is as statistics which helps draw comparisons between numerical quantities; another form is as **diagrams**, which helps make these quantities easier to understand. There are different types of diagrams and the one used depends upon the type of quantity to be represented. This is illustrated in Fig. 1.1.

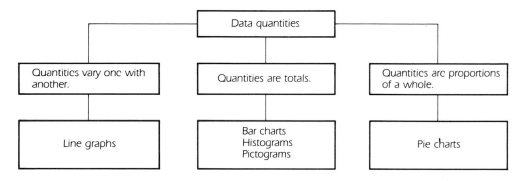

Fig. 1.1

Line Graphs

Line graphs are generally used to show the variations between two quantities, such as time/distance, temperature/time, current/voltage, or profit/sales. A graph is a picture showing numerical information.

They have two **axes**, the horizontal and the vertical, and the point where the axes cross is known as the **origin** (O). What the axes show has to be carefully selected, and clearly labelled. A grid drawn with fine lines helps to guide the eye.

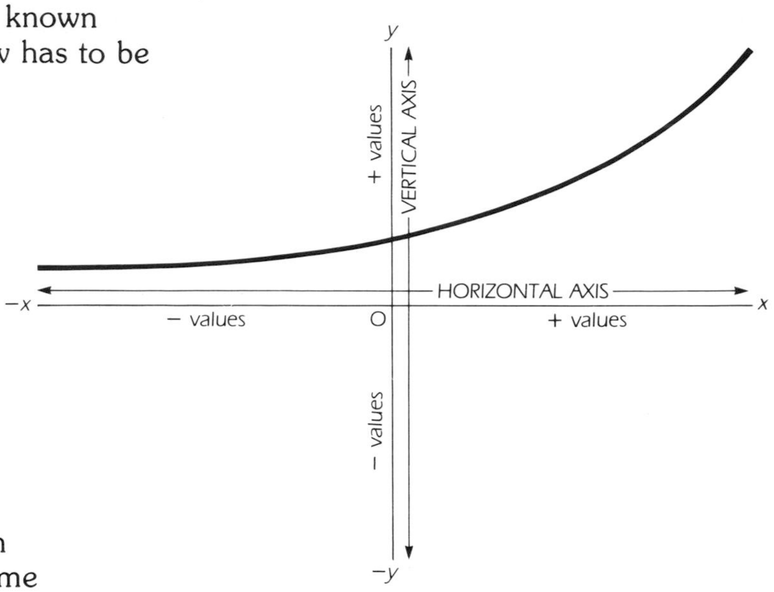

Small dots are used to mark the plotted points and these are joined together with clearly defined straight or curved lines. When there is more than one line on the same base, the lines are identified by colour or various types of broken line, and a key is added. It is important when drawing a graph to select a sensible scale. The scale on a graph is the spacing between the labels on the axes.

Fig. 1.2

Fig. 1.3 shows a graph on which all the numbers are positive (greater than zero).

A graph must always have a **title** positioned at the top (like 'Average monthly temperature' on Fig. 1.3). It is also important when drawing a graph to select a **scale** that makes the graph a convenient size and not condensed, and the scale on the graph should always be spaced evenly, with the units clearly defined. The **trend** or slope of the graph can be exaggerated or diminished by bad selection of scales.

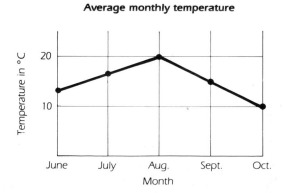

Fig. 1.3

The coordinates say where the points are on a graph.
The point P in Fig. 1.4 has coordinates (4, 3). The first number, 4,
says how far along horizontally the point is positioned. The second
number, 3, says how far up vertically the point is positioned.

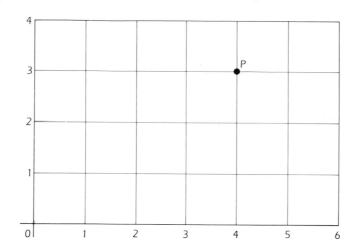

Fig. 1.4

EXERCISES

1. Give the coordinates of the points A, B, C, D, E, F, G, H, I, J, K and L. Copy the
   graph on to squared paper and draw a smooth curve through the points.

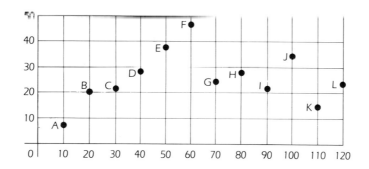

Fig. 1.5

2. A car was tested for petrol consumption at various speeds.

Speed in mph	10	20	30	50	56	70	80
Petrol consumption in mpg	20	35	38	39	41	36	24

Plot the points and draw a smooth curve through them.
State the petrol consumption at 40 mph.
At what speed is the petrol consumption 25 mpg?
What is the most efficient speed at which to drive the car?

3. *Fig. 1.6 illustrates a slope of* $\dfrac{30 \text{ miles}}{1 \text{ hour}}$ *= 30 mph.*

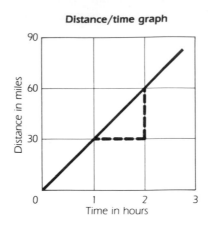

Distance/time graph

Fig. 1.6

a) Find the slope of the graph in Fig. 1.7 during the first three seconds.

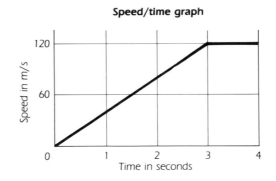

Speed/time graph

Fig. 1.7

b) Find the gradient of the graph in Fig. 1.8.

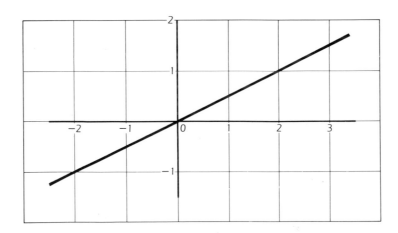

Fig. 1.8

Bar Charts

There are three types of **bar chart**:

- a **single bar**,
- a **vertical bar**, and
- a **horizontal bar**.

When presenting information in the form of charts, graphs or maps there are three basic things that have to be decided upon:

- what information has to be presented,
- to whom the information is to be presented, and
- what scale is to be used.

Axes of charts have to be selected very carefully. The **trend** of the chart can be exaggerated or diminished by the bad selection of scales.

All charts must have both the scales and the units clearly defined.

All charts must have titles.

All axes on charts must be suitably labelled.

EXAMPLE

A family has a monthly income of £600 and spends it in the following way:

Food £200

Clothing £100

Heating £40

Lighting £40

Rates and mortgage £180

Other expenses £40

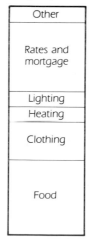

Monthly expenditure

Scale: 10 mm represents £100

Fig. 1.9

This information can be shown on a single bar chart as in Fig. 1.9, a vertical bar chart as in Fig. 1.10, or a horizontal bar chart as in Fig. 1.11 (see overleaf).

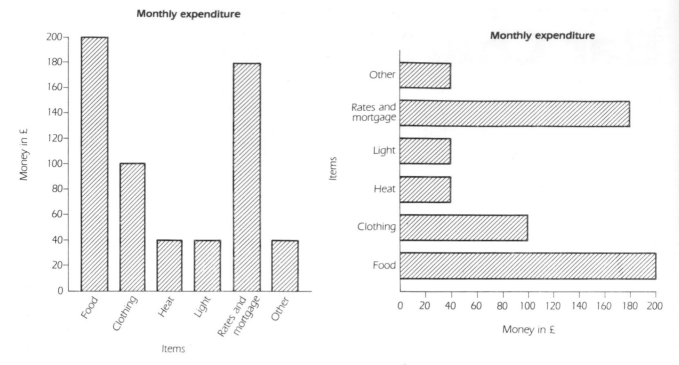

Fig. 1.10   **Fig. 1.11**

On a single bar chart (Fig. 1.9), the heights of the different sections illustrate how much is spent upon each item in relation to the other items. The lengths of the individual sections show clearly how much is spent.

EXERCISES

1. *A new range of hacksaw blades has recently been marketed and a sample survey has been carried out on the consumer market. 500 engineers have been questioned. 260 said that they preferred the original type of blade; 140 said that they liked the way in which the new blades fitted into the existing handles; 40 liked the variable teeth; 15 preferred the new way of marking the direction of cut; and 45 liked the new blades and said that they would consider using them in the future.*
    Draw a bar chart to illustrate the above information.

2. *The horizontal bar chart in Fig. 1.12 shows how the sales of two new oil products have varied between 1980 and 1984. Study the chart and answer the questions that follow.*

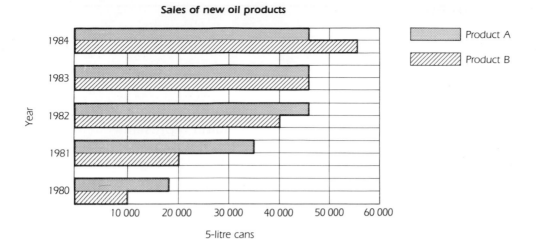

Sales of new oil products

Fig. 1.12

a) Which was the most popular oil product in 1980, product A or product B?
b) Was product A or product B more popular in 1984?
c) How many litres of product B were sold in 1982?
d) How many litres more were used of product A in 1984 than in 1981?
e) Would the manufacturer have done better to have concentrated upon a high sales and promotional programme for product B in 1981?

3. According to Fig. 1.13, how many hours of sunshine can be expected in England on a day in November?

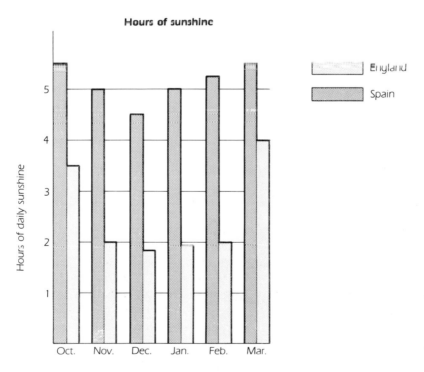

Hours of sunshine

Fig. 1.13

[AEB, 1985]

Histograms

A **histogram** is a graph in which the area of the column represents the **frequency** of an occurrence (the number of times it happens). The simplest type of histogram is a bar chart in which all the bars are of the same width.

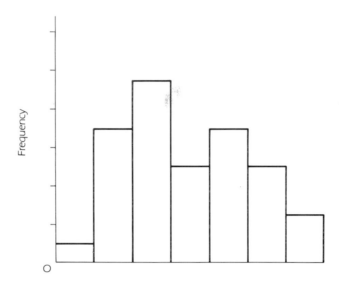

Fig. 1.14

EXAMPLE

The diameters of 50 ball bearings were measured and their measurements were recorded as follows, with the view of ensuring that the manufacturing process was within the tolerance of 24.00 mm plus or minus 0.01 mm.

23.99	24.02	24.00	24.00	23.98
24.00	24.00	23.99	24.00	24.00
24.01	23.99	24.00	23.99	24.00
24.00	24.01	24.00	24.00	24.00
24.01	24.02	23.99	24.00	24.01
23.99	24.00	24.00	24.01	24.00
23.98	24.02	24.00	23.99	24.00
24.01	24.01	24.00	24.00	24.00
24.00	24.00	23.99	24.00	23.99
23.99	24.00	24.00	24.00	23.99

As these numbers stand they have little clear meaning, but if the measurements are grouped together in a **frequency table** (see opposite page) it will be possible to see a pattern emerging.

Measurement	Tally			Frequency
23.98	II			2
23.99	JHT	JHT	I	11
24.00	JHT	JHT	JHT	
	JHT	JHT	II	27
24.01	JHT	II		7
24.02	III			3

A **tally** mark is simply a way of counting. Every time a measurement of, for example, 23.98 is counted a mark is put into the tally column against 23.98. Every fifth mark is drawn across a group of four. The frequency of a measurement is the number of marks that appears against it.

The results can then be displayed on a histogram. In this case, it can be seen quite clearly from the chart in Fig. 1.15 that the most frequent measurement occurring is 24.00 mm, with a sharp falling-off on either side. This indicates that the manufacturing process must be fairly accurate.

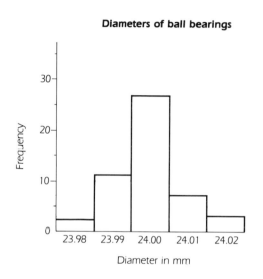

Fig. 1.15

If the histogram looked like Fig. 1.16, it would be obvious that the manufacturing process was at fault. Steps would have to be taken in order to remedy the fault in the process.

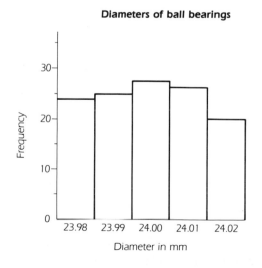

Fig. 1.16

EXERCISES

1. The lengths of 42 steel bars were measured and the measurements recorded. All the measurements are in millimetres.

83.95	83.98	83.95	83.96	83.94	83.94
83.94	83.92	83.95	83.94	83.93	83.96
83.95	83.96	83.97	83.93	83.95	83.95
83.95	83.96	83.97	83.97	83.92	83.94
83.96	83.96	83.94	83.98	83.00	83.99
84.00	83.99	83.94	83.96	83.97	83.94
83.98	83.97	83.96	83.94	83.99	83.97

    Draw up a frequency table and from that draw a histogram.

2. The histogram in Fig. 1.17 shows the stock held in six boxes in a store room.
    Which box holds the most stock?
    Which box holds the least stock?
    Approximately how much stock is there in total in six boxes?

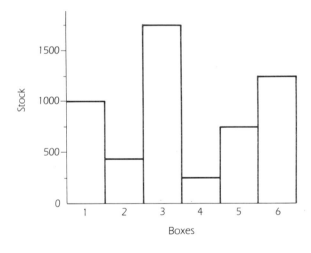

Stock held in six boxes

Fig. 1.17

3. Six unbiased two pence pieces are spun. The results are as follows.

Class	Frequency
6 heads	2
5 heads, 1 tail	12
4 heads, 2 tails	30
3 heads, 3 tails	40
2 heads, 4 tails	30
1 head, 5 tails	14
6 tails	2

    Draw a histogram to illustrate these figures.

Pie Charts

A **pie chart** is a useful way of being able to show numerical information in the form of a picture. The whole is represented as a **circle**, with the various elements represented as **sectors** whose size is proportional to the value of the elements.

EXAMPLE

24 engineers were asked when they would like to take their holidays.

8 said that they would like to take their holidays during the summer.

3 chose to take their holidays during the winter.

2 said that they would take their holidays in the spring.

5 said they would prefer an autumn holiday.

The remainder were specific and said that they would like to go on a skiing holiday together, taking the last week in January and the first week in February.

Fig. 1.18 shows this information on a pie chart.

Constructing a pie chart

1 Draw a conveniently sized circle with a compass.
2 Calculate the angles at the centre of the circle, and put the information in a table.
3 Use a protractor to measure the angles, and draw them.
4 Label each sector.
5 Indicate the angles on the pie chart.

Holiday preferences

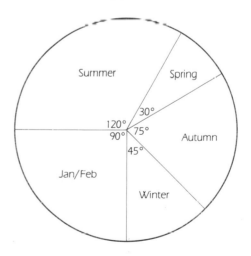

Fig. 1.18

Calculating the angles in the centre of a pie chart

There are 360° in a circle, and these have to be divided by the number of elements that are to be included in the chart (in this case 24). This will then give the angle per element. In some examples the number will have to be rounded up or down to the nearest whole degree.

To find the angle of each section, multiply this number by the number of elements in each section.

This is shown in the table below.

360 divided by 24 equals 15, so there are 15° per element.

Sector label	Number of elements (engineers)	Angle
Summer	8	8 × 15 = 120°
Winter	3	3 × 15 = 45°
Spring	2	2 × 15 = 30°
Autumn	5	5 × 15 = 75°
Jan/Feb	6	6 × 15 = 90°

N.B. It is often not possible to draw a pie chart completely accurately because the thickness of the lines you draw might take up half a degree or so.

EXERCISES

1. *A pupil spends £1.28 a week in the manner illustrated by the pie chart in Fig. 1.19. How much does he spend on magazines? How much does he spend on sweets, and how much does he put in his bank as savings?*
   He also enjoys watching and supporting his local football club and allows a certain amount of money each week for this purpose. How much?

Pupil's weekly expenditure

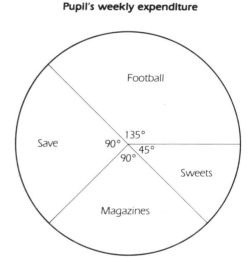

Fig. 1.19

2. *A family spends the following amounts of money on the general cost of living each week. Illustrate this data as a pie chart.*

Food	*£24*
Services	*£12*
Rates	*£14*
Clothing	*£12*
Petrol	*£7*

3. Draw a pie chart illustrating the proportion of different types of trees that are growing on Shotover Hill, given the following data.

Scots pine	120	Larch	45
Ash	45	Hazel	60
Oak	90		

4. The following table states the distances that a class of school pupils have to travel every day in order to attend school.

	Less than 1 mile	1.25 miles	2.6 miles	Over 5 miles
Number of pupils	10	22	11	7

What is the total number of pupils taking part in the survey?
What angle on a pie chart would represent one pupil?
Complete a frequency table for the information presented. Draw a pie chart to represent it, marking on the angles.

5. A pupil made a study of how she spent her time watching television one day. She found that 60 minutes were spent watching comedy, 72 minutes watching sport programmes, 9 minutes watching the news and 23 minutes watching quiz programmes. The remaining 16 minutes were occupied with the advertisements on commercial television.
Make a table of the information presented.
How many minutes have been spent watching television? Convert this into hours.
Draw a pie chart to represent the information. What angle will represent each minute of watching time on the pie chart?
Are you able to describe the pupil's likes and dislikes from this study?

6. A local authority has conducted a survey of the traffic using a particular roundabout, which is shown in Fig. 1.20, and wants to determine which priorities to give to a road widening scheme. There are five exit roads and a dual carriageway leading to a nearby motorway. The percentage of vehicles coming from the motorway which leave by each of the five exit roads is as follows.

To London via the old road 42%

To the north of the city 24%

To the west of the city 17%

To the south of the city 7%

To the east of the city 10%

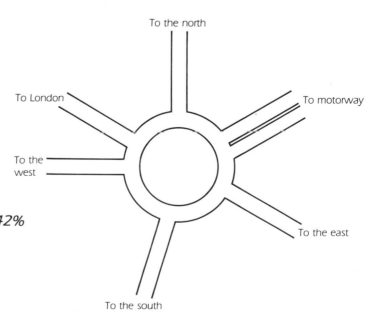

Fig. 1.20

Draw a pie chart to illustrate the volume of traffic using the five exits other than the dual carriageway that leads to the motorway.

Using an alternative graphical method represent the percentage of traffic that is using each of the five exits.

7. Europe is a popular place for British holidaymakers. Listed below are the numbers of visitors to each country.

Country	Tourists	Country	Tourists
Austria	3 000 000	Portugal	4 000 000
Belgium	1 000 000	Spain	21 000 000
France	18 000 000	Switzerland	2 000 000
Greece	6 000 000	West Germany	2 000 000
Italy	7 000 000		

Trace the map of Europe in Fig. 1.21 and on the outline illustrate, using a graphical method, the flow of tourists to each country in a way that shows a comparison between the numbers.

Draw an alternative graph, diagram or chart to represent the number of tourists taking holidays in the different countries.

Fig. 1.21

SPECIAL USES: BREAKDOWNS

Pie charts are especially useful as visual representations of the
breakdown of various problems. Fig. 1.22 is a typical example of
how they can be used in a beneficial way in industry.

Concrete mixes for DIY jobs

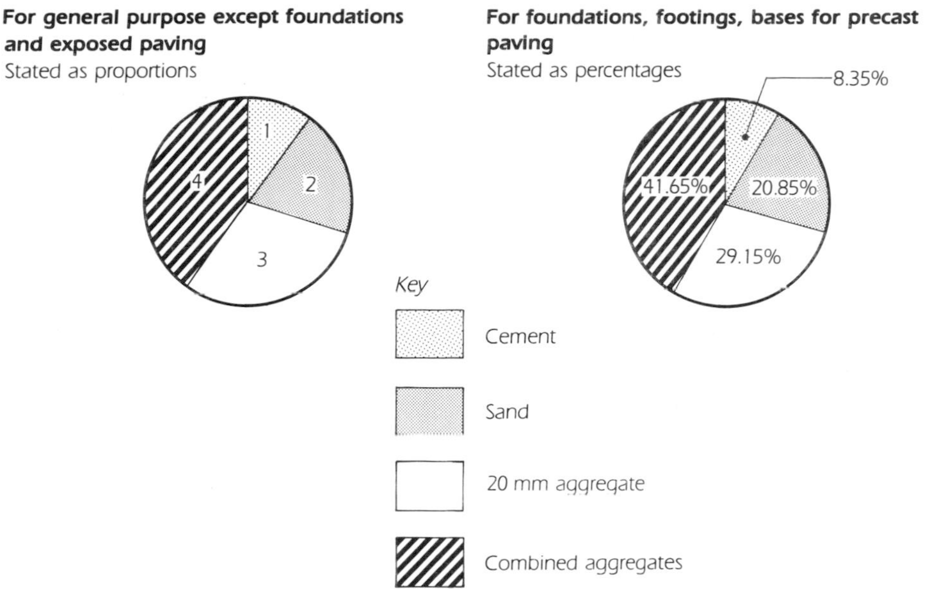

**For general purpose except foundations
and exposed paving**
Stated as proportions

**For foundations, footings, bases for precast
paving**
Stated as percentages

8.35%

41.65%   20.85%

29.15%

Key

Cement

Sand

20 mm aggregate

Combined aggregates

Fig. 1.22

EXERCISES

1. *The motor car in Fig. 1.23 is divided up to illustrate the costs involved in its production
    (excluding labour).*
    Represent this data as a pie chart.

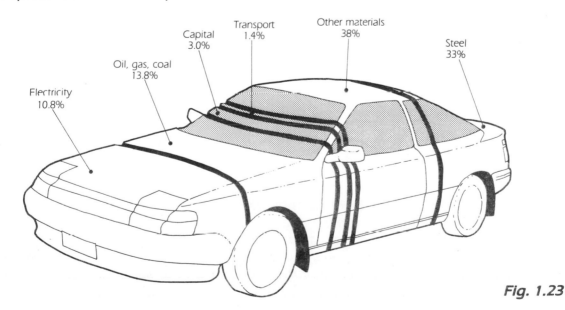

Transport
1.4%

Capital
3.0%

Other materials
38%

Steel
33%

Oil, gas, coal
13.8%

Electricity
10.8%

Fig. 1.23

2. *The loaf of bread in Fig. 1.24 is divided up in a manner that shows the costs involved (excluding labour) in order to produce and retail one loaf.*
Represent this data as a pie chart.

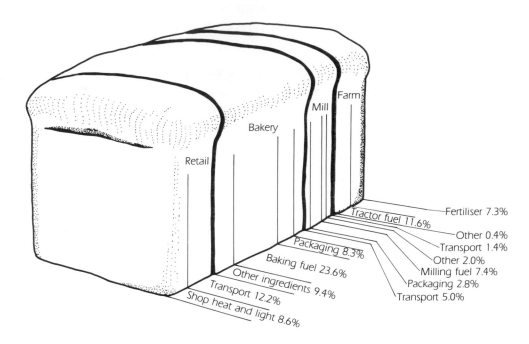

Retail

Bakery

Mill

Farm

Fertiliser 7.3%

Tractor fuel 11.6%

Other 0.4%

Transport 1.4%

Other 2.0%

Milling fuel 7.4%

Packaging 2.8%

Transport 5.0%

Packaging 8.3%

Baking fuel 23.6%

Other ingredients 9.4%

Transport 12.2%

Shop heat and light 8.6%

Fig. 1.24

3. *An Area Health Authority is concerned by the increasing number of accidents to children which occur in the home. In one year the Authority's group of hospitals recorded the following accidents, to children aged between 10 and 14 years, which were serious enough to require treatment.*

Home accidents: age 10–14 years

Location	Number	%
Kitchen	601	13.5
Bathroom/toilet	84	1.9
Living/dining room	642	14.4
Bedroom	358	8.0
Inside stairs	397	8.9
Hall	156	3.5
Garden/outside area	899	20.2
Garage	565	12.6
Other	487	10.9
Unknown	268	6.1
TOTAL	4457	100.0

It has been decided to promote a publicity campaign to reduce this accident rate by drawing attention to the number of accidents, the ages of the children involved, and the locations of the danger areas in the home. Charts which illustrate these statistics are required.
Design a graphic representation of the statistical data to illustrate a magazine article on 'Accidents in the home'.

[OLE]

4. *Fig. 1.25 represents the braking efficiency of Austin Seven motor cars manufactured between 1929 and 1936, taken from the road tests published by Autocar magazine.*

    Construct a pie chart to illustrate the braking efficiency of each model while travelling at 30 miles per hour.

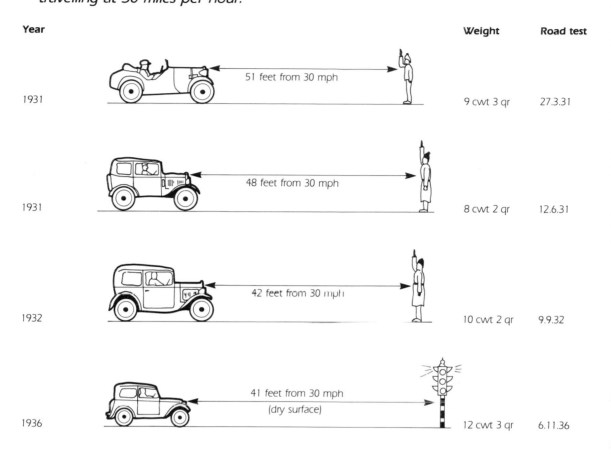

Year		Weight	Road test
1931	51 feet from 30 mph	9 cwt 3 qr	27.3.31
1931	48 feet from 30 mph	8 cwt 2 qr	12.6.31
1932	42 feet from 30 mph	10 cwt 2 qr	9.9.32
1936	41 feet from 30 mph (dry surface)	12 cwt 3 qr	6.11.36

Weights indicated are less passengers

Fig. 1.25

5. *Energy consumption is an important feature of our daily lives. The table below sets out the energy requirements for Katie, mass 45 kg, over a 24-hour period.*

Activity	Hours	Energy needed/ hour (kcal/hour)	= Energy used (kcal)
Sleeping	8	66	528
Sitting	4	84	336
Light work (sitting)	4	150	600
Light work (standing)	5	180	900
Moderate work	2	300	600
Hard work	1	450	450

Total energy requirement 3414

Construct a pie chart to show this information.

Operations in Sequence

The ideal set of instructions for a **sequence of operations** that one could present to anybody would be in a pictorial form showing sketches of the details of everything that is to be used – perhaps a drawing board and T-square with the paper being held on to the board with two board clips to illustrate 'drawing'. This would help overcome any language barrier that could exist.

Some things, however, would be difficult to draw, and different people could interpret the sketches in different ways. In any case, picture language is extremely space consuming and takes a long time to draw, so it is better to make presentation clearer by reducing as much as possible to symbols without being at all ambiguous.

EXAMPLE

When teaching a child the kerb drill for crossing the road, the instructions below could be given in a diagram like the one in Fig. 1.26.

1   Listen. Is there any traffic noise indicating that there is a motor vehicle nearby?
2   Wait at the edge of the kerb.
3   Look right.
4   Look left.
5   Look right again.
6   Is there any traffic approaching?
7   If yes, wait.
8   Is there any traffic approaching?
9   If no:
10 Step off from the kerb.
11 Keep looking as you cross.
12 Reach the other side of the road.

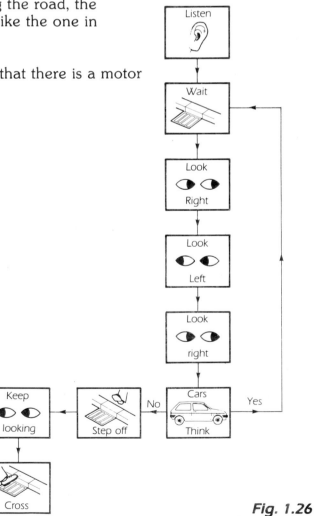

Fig. 1.26

SIMPLE PICTURES SHOWING OPERATIONS IN SEQUENCE

Austin Rover have a Press Line monitoring system and through the graphic illustration in Fig. 1.27 we are able to appreciate how it functions.

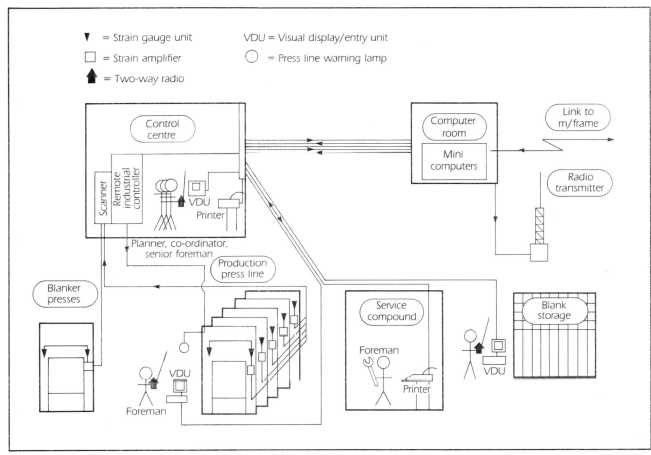

Fig. 1.27

Since installing the Byker plant in Doncaster, the Refuse Department concentrates on manufacturing waste-derived fuel pellets. All the materials that do not go into the fuel pellets, except metal, are used for land infill. See Fig. 1.28

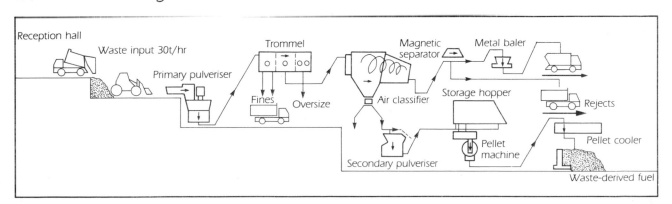

Fig. 1.28

EXERCISES

1. *Present the following sequence of instructions as a series of diagrams with brief captions of the processes involved in making custard. The first diagram has been completed for you in Fig. 1.29.*

   a) *Into a basin put two tablespoons of sugar and two tablespoons of custard powder.*

   b) *Mix slowly with two tablespoons of cold milk.*

   c) *Place a saucepan into which is poured one pint of milk on a source of heat and heat until near boiling point.*

   d) *Pour the nearly boiling milk on to the custard and stir well.*

   e) *Return the custard to the saucepan and bring to the boil stirring all the time.*

   f) *The custard is now ready to serve.*

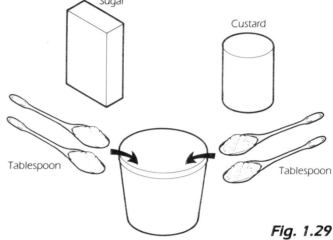

Fig. 1.29

2. *Illustrate the following process in terms of a graphical sequence.*

   A soldered contact has to be made to a fixed terminal on an electric motor using a low voltage electric soldering iron, flux and multicored solder. The wire has to be stripped initially of its braiding. The bared wires have to be twisted together and then fluxed. The soldering iron has to be plugged into the socket and the socket switched on, and when the iron has reached the required heat the twisted end of the wire has to be tinned. The motor terminal has to be cleaned with emery cloth and tinned, and then the wire must be attached to the terminal and finally soldered.

3. *Illustrate the following details using the **operations in sequence** means of graphical representation.*

   A piece of mild steel bar has to be turned on a centre lathe to the specification illustrated in Fig. 1.30. Initially the bar is a length of mild steel of diameter 25 mm and length 150 mm.

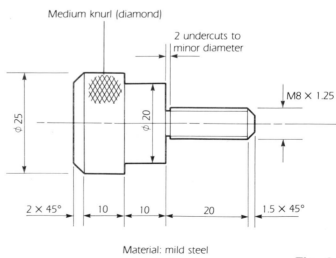

Material: mild steel
All dimensions in mm

Fig. 1.30

4. *Illustrate the following processes in terms of a graphical sequence.*
A mortice and tenon joint has to be cut on a piece of parana pine to the dimensions given in Fig. 1.31. Show clearly the various stages and the tools that are to be used in producing this joint.

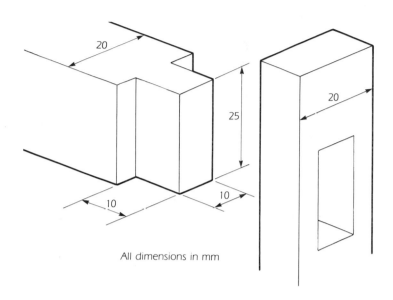

All dimensions in mm

Fig. 1.31

5. *Describe graphically, with limited use of written notes, how the handle of a hacksaw is to be produced in an engineering workshop to the specification prescribed in Fig. 1.32, from a blank piece of bright mild steel GCQ (General Commercial Quality) 125 mm by 100 mm by 5 mm.*

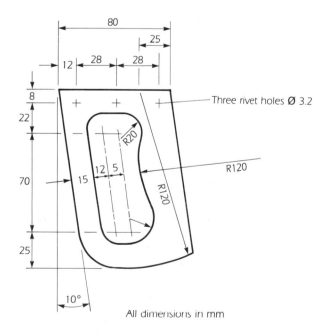

All dimensions in mm

Fig. 1.32

DIAGRAMMATIC REPRESENTATION – THE SYSTEM APPROACH

As we have seen in this chapter, it is useful to be able to illustrate a series of activities and processes, using signs and symbols to eliminate a vast quantity of words.

A natural progression is to move on to a standard system. Initially we are looking for a simple means of describing a flow of activities in a logical sequence. One valuable way of doing this is by means of block diagrams. This system is called the **black box system** and is simply a series of boxes with inputs, outputs and the details of the activity inside the box.

The system approach is a strategy for understanding complex situations, and for arriving at solutions to problems arising from these complex situations. It is a way of breaking down a system into a number of component parts and making clear their inter-relationships. At the same time it may reveal gaps in the system which would lead to unsatisfactory behaviour.

Many people have the idea that system analyses, often known as flow charts, are something special and directly allied to computing. This is not so; they do not involve computer programming at all. They provide a logical way of planning and drawing step-by-step solutions to a problem.

Consider the flow in Fig. 1.33 that takes place from buying some cooking apples at your local supermarket to finally eating them.

Buying, cooking and eating apples

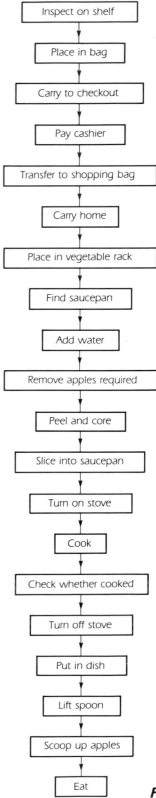

Fig. 1.33

A system approach to an investigational project

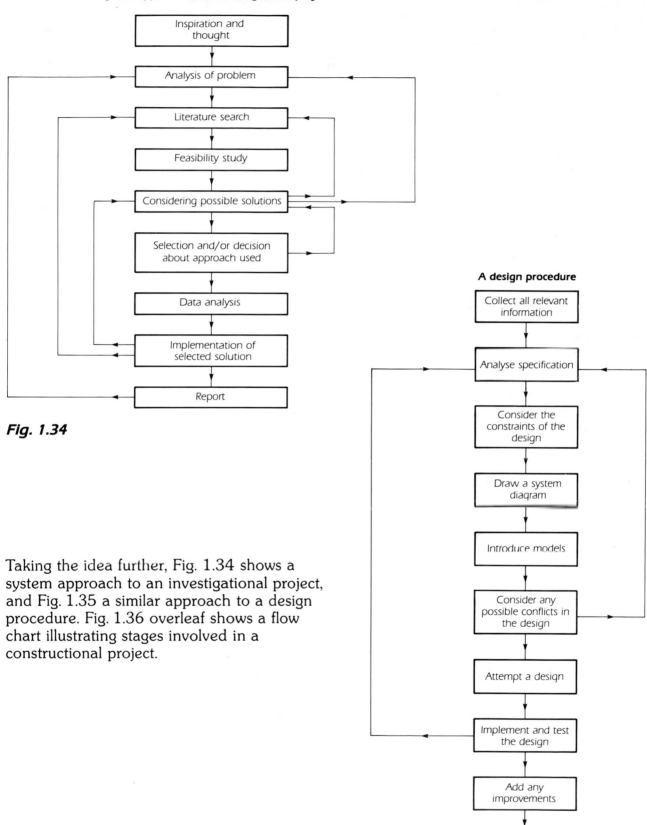

Fig. 1.34

Taking the idea further, Fig. 1.34 shows a system approach to an investigational project, and Fig. 1.35 a similar approach to a design procedure. Fig. 1.36 overleaf shows a flow chart illustrating stages involved in a constructional project.

A design procedure

Fig. 1.35

Stages involved in undertaking a constructional project

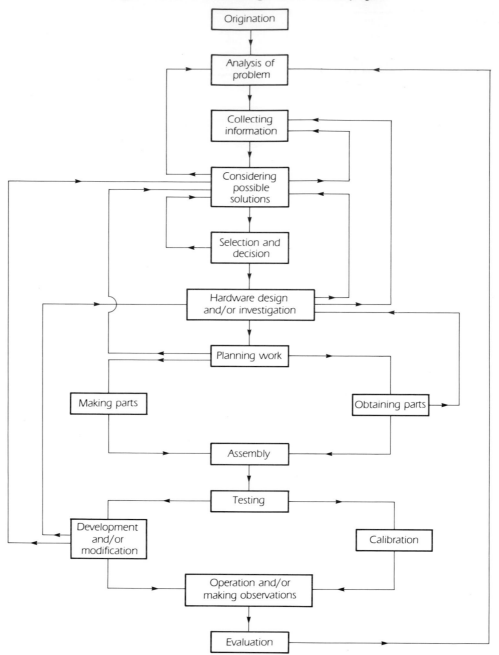

Fig. 1.36

EXERCISES

1. *Fig. 1.37 shows the sequence in supplying water and flushing a wc. Translate the diagram into a suitable drawing which clearly shows the necessary components.*

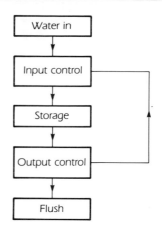

Fig. 1.37

2. *The stages in washing your hands are shown, but listed in the wrong order. Illustrate the stages in the correct order as a diagrammatic representation.*
   a) *Run hot water.*
   b) *Is the temperature correct?*
   c) *Put plug in basin.*
   d) *Wash hands.*
   e) *Remove plug from basin.*
   f) *Add liquid soap.*
   g) *Run cold water.*

3. *Complete the black box system diagram (Fig. 1.38) illustrating the relationship between the use of public transport and a rise in the number of car owners.*

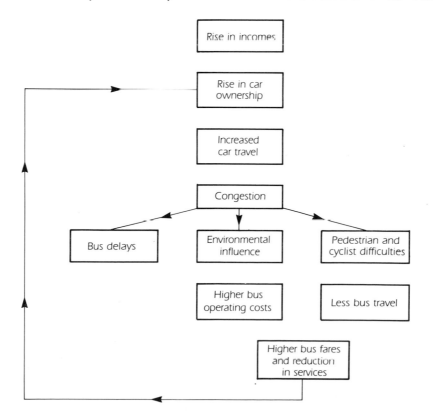

Fig. 1.38

Flow Diagrams

Having worked through diagrammatic representation, we shall now consider using a chart in which symbols drawn in a particular way act as a form of instruction.

Flow diagrams have mainly been developed for business and computer applications, where certain actions have to be carried out in a particular order. Fig. 1.39 shows these symbols, with each symbol's specific meaning. The direction of flow along a series of operations can be shown by flow diagrams. The shapes are joined by arrows to indicate the direction of travel, with sign-posts based on 'yes' and 'no' answers to questions.

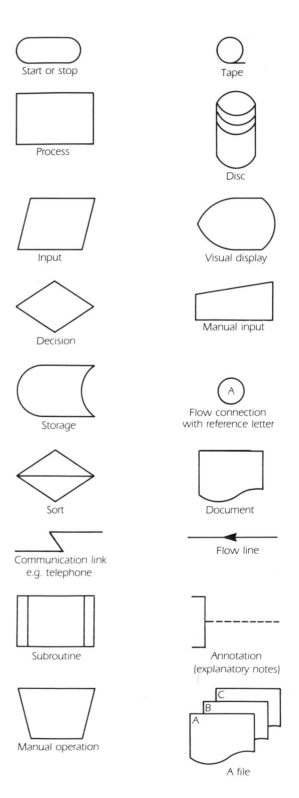

Fig. 1.39

EXAMPLE

Listed below are the various operations that are undertaken when refilling a cartridge pen that is in your pocket.

  1   Does the pen require refilling?
  2   Remove the pen from your pocket.
  3   Unscrew the cap from the barrel.
  4   Unscrew the barrel from the nib holder.
  5   Remove the spent cartridge.
  6   Insert the new cartridge.
  7   Screw the barrel into the nib holder.
  8   Test for the flow of ink.
  9   Adjust if necessary.
 10   Use the pen.
 11   Replace the cap on the barrel.
 12   Replace the pen in your pocket.

Study the flow diagram in Fig. 1.40 and associate the different symbols with the processes set out above.

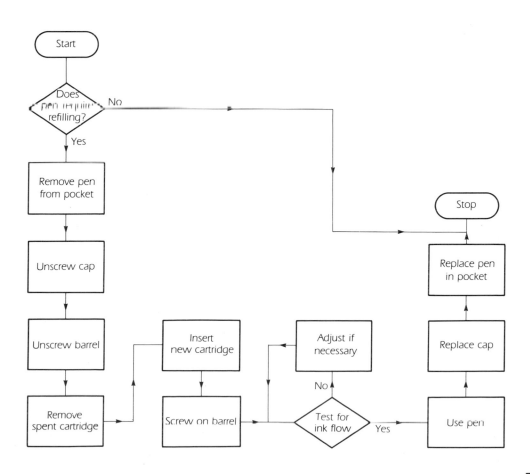

Fig. 1.40

You will have noticed that start and stop boxes are rectangular with rounded ends, and instruction boxes rectangular or square. A diamond-shaped box indicates that decisions have to be made. They have two exits, one for 'yes' and one for 'no', allowing different paths to be taken through the flow chart. There are often 'loops' which permit certain instructions to be repeated. Looking at Fig. 1.40 you will appreciate that the chart commences at 'start' and finishes at 'stop', but it is not necessary to follow all the paths, only the ones that are required. The loops put in can send you backwards so that an operation may be repeated – in this case adjusting the ink flow. Loops are very important in drawing flow diagrams, but it is important to make sure there is a way of escaping so that you do not travel around in continuous circles.

Fig. 1.41 shows a program for collecting information from the resource room. The flow chart illustrates the processes that you will go through when you are finding information required for a project.

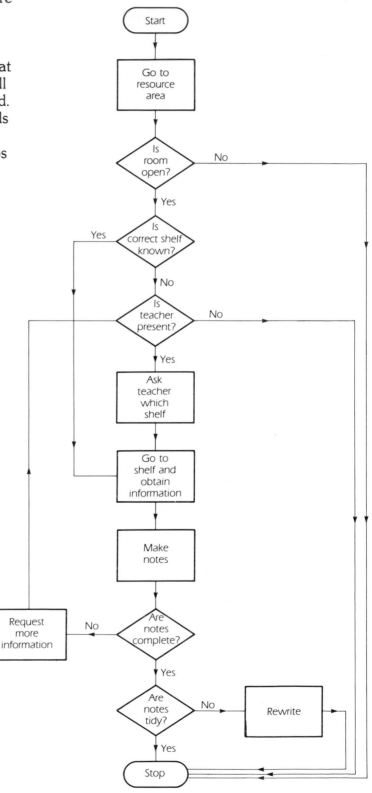

Fig. 1.41

Fig. 1.42 is the flow diagram for a computer program for an addition game, using more advanced symbols.

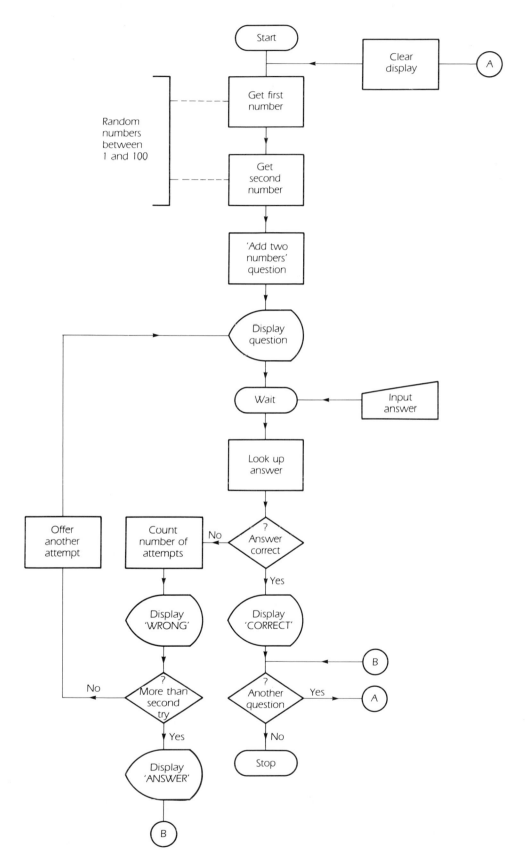

Fig. 1.42

EXERCISES

Construct flow diagrams for the following operations.

1. Doing the necessary preparatory work prior to drilling a 6 mm hole through a 3 mm piece of steel on a drilling machine.

2. Sharpening a wood chisel on an oilstone.

3. Forming a piece of plastic over a former on a simple hand-operated vacuum forming machine.

4. Attaching drawing paper to the drawing board.
   a) Place paper near the top left-hand corner of the drawing board.
   b) Remove one board clip from the instrument box.
   c) Place clip on the left-hand corner of the paper.
   d) Remove a second clip from the instrument box.
   e) Place second clip on the right-hand corner of the paper.
   f) Check that the paper is square using a T-square.
   g) Adjust the paper if necessary.

5. Tying up shoe laces.
   a) Place one foot in a shoe.
   b) Hold the right-hand end of the lace in the right hand.
   c) Hold the left-hand end of the lace in the left hand.
   d) Tie a half hitch.
   e) Form a loop in the left hand.
   f) Wind the right hand lace around the loop.
   g) Pull a loop from the right-hand end through the loop you have just formed.
   h) Pull the two loops tightly together using both hands.

6. Drawing a straight line using a pencil and a T-square.
   a) Hold the T-square firmly against the edge of the drawing board.
   b) Pick up a pencil and hold between the thumb and forefinger.
   c) Draw the pencil along the T-square top edge revolving the pencil slowly.
   d) Lift off the pencil at the end of the line.

7. Unlocking a house door fitted with a 'Yale' type of lock.
   a) Remove the key from your pocket.
   b) Place the key in the lock.
   c) Turn the key towards the right.
   d) Push the door open.
   e) Remove the key from the lock.
   f) Replace the key in pocket.

8. Selecting a stamp from a stamp book.
   a) Open the stamp book.
   b) Decide if the letter has to be sent by first or second class mail.
   c) Turn to the first page of stamps and decide if the stamps are the correct value.
   d) If the stamps are of the correct value, tear out a stamp from the booklet.
   e) Lick the reverse face of the stamp.
   f) Place the stamp upon the envelope in the top right-hand corner.
   g) If value is incorrect, turn over to the next page of stamps, and repeat from d.

9. A casting is made by packing a pattern in sand in a moulding box, the lower box being known as the drag and the upper box as the cope. The two parts of the box are separated, the pattern is removed and the mould finally prepared for casting. Aluminium is charged into the crucible which is placed in the furnace until the aluminium melts. The slag is then removed from the melt and the metal is poured into the mould. When the casting is cool it is then knocked out of the mould, fettled and sent to the machine shop for finishing.

The activities involved in preparing a mould for casting are listed below.

Arrange them in a logical sequence in the form of a flow diagram.

a) Place inverted drag on the moulding board.

b) Place half pattern in the centre of the inverted drag.

c) Dust the pattern with parting powder.

d) Riddle over the pattern with prepared green sand.

e) Ram green sand into the remaining space until level with the bottom of the drag.

f) Strickle off.

g) Turn the drag the right way up.

h) Place the upper part of the split pattern on the lower portion in the drag.

i) Position the cope accurately on the drag.

j) Dust with parting powder.

k) Position the sprue pins.

l) Repeat the activities d, e and f.

m) Complete infilling until green sand is level with the top of the cope.

n) Cut a pouring basin.

o) Using bellows, blow off any excess sand.

p) Gently rap the sprue pins.

q) Remove the sprue pins from the mould.

r) Separate the cope and the drag.

s) Insert removal pins into each section of the pattern in the cope and the drag.

t) Rap the removal pins gently.

u) Remove the two sections of split pattern from the cope and the drag.

v) Repair the mould if necessary.

w) Position the cope on the top of the drag.

x) Cover the cope with a moulding board to prevent dust and possible damage.

10. A local foundry produces aluminium gearbox castings. There are three castings that make up the complete case. After the case components are cast they are then sent to the machine shop where all the machining is carried out, such as milling, trepanning, line boring, drilling and tapping.

The processes are termed 1, 2, 3, 4, 5, 6, 6a, 7, 7a, 8, 8a, and 8b.

Construct a flow chart from the following information.

The three castings C1, C2, and C3 start at 1 (checking), and then C1 passes to 2 (marking out) and then on to 6. C2 passes to 3 (removing flashing) and then on to 5. C3 passes to 4 (marking out), then on to 6a (trepanning) and then on to 7 (milling).

When the milling processes 5 and 6 have been completed castings C1 and C2 are then drilled and tapped (7a). Casting C3 is drilled (8a) after the line boring is completed (8). The complete machining processes are checked (8b). The final products are then sent to the assembly department and the faulty products are returned to the foundry.

Bar Codes

The **bar code system** is part of a scheme that covers most of the Western world giving retailed products a unique and unambiguous identifying system through numbers. Bar codes are used on groceries, toiletries and many other products – there is one on the back of this book. The system means that every product, and every variation of the product in terms of size, colour and retailing details, carries its own unique number, allowing the retailer to send orders directly to the supplier via a computer. This provides a universally understood means of communication. The scheme is designed to give a faster and generally better method of communication from the manufacturing to the retail outlets, and is administered in this country by the Article Number Association (UK) Ltd.

The bar code is a **machine readable** form of the unique number that is given to a specific product. The international system uses a 13-digit number. The first two (or sometimes 3) digits identify the nationality of the number bank issuing that specific number; the next five (or sometimes 4) numbers are allocated to a particular manufacturer or supplier; and the following five numbers identify the product. The final digit is a check digit to ensure that the code is correctly composed. It has a mathematical relationship to the other numbers, ensuring that if any mistake has been made in composing the first 12 digits, the computer will instantly alert the operator that the number is incorrect.

To make this 13-digit number machine readable it is coded as a series of bars and spaces. The number appears underneath the bar code with the first digit to the left and positioned outside the bars. The code starts and ends with two longer and thinner bars, and two similar bars separate the code into left-hand and right-hand parts. There are always 24 other bars in a code, which vary in width and spacing according to a predetermined structure.

STRUCTURE

Study the code in Fig. 1.43.

5 012345 678900   **Fig. 1.43**

On the right-hand side you will see that there are six digits and 12 dark bars, and each of the digits is associated with a pair of the bars. You will notice if you examine a range of products that 0 is always represented on the left-hand side by a particular pattern of two bars, as in the example of a bar code used by Uhu on their gluepens shown in Fig. 1.44.

5 000199 026114   **Fig. 1.44**

THE CHECK DIGIT

When the system was first introduced in the United States the originators considered that 12 digits would be sufficient, but when it was adopted internationally it was found that this was not fully practical. It was felt necessary to encode an extra digit to provide a check, using the 12 which were already there. This was done by having two different representations for each of the digits 0 to 9 for the left-hand part of the code. These are known as the **A and B representations**. A mixture of A and B representations can be used on the left-hand side, and the particular permutation of the As and Bs selected is the code for the thirteenth digit.

All the patterns for the digits are constructed upon seven units of equal width. Fig. 1.45 shows a representation for 0. The first three units are dark, the next two are light, the following one dark and the final one light.

Fig. 1.45

It must be possible to distinguish the boundary between one digit and the next, so the first unit of one digit must be different from the seventh of the digit before it. On the right-hand side the first unit is always dark and the last is always light. On the left-hand side, for both the A and B patterns, the converse is always true. Fig 1.46 illustrates the three representations for 0. Compare the A and B representations of 0 on the left-hand side of Fig. 1.46, and the representation on the right-hand side.

Left A   Left B   Right

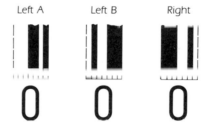

Fig. 1.46

EXERCISES

1. *Make a collection of typical packaging and identify on it the code for the UK.*

2. *Some products apparently made by different companies have identical manufacturers' references. Can you suggest why?*

3. *Are different sizes of the same product given different numbers?*

4. *Are revised forms of packaging given the same code as the packaging originally used?*

5. *How wide can a bar be in terms of units?*

ARTICLE NUMBERING WORLD-WIDE

On the world map in Fig. 1.47 the numbers that are marked
represent the initial digits of article numbers issued in that particular
country.

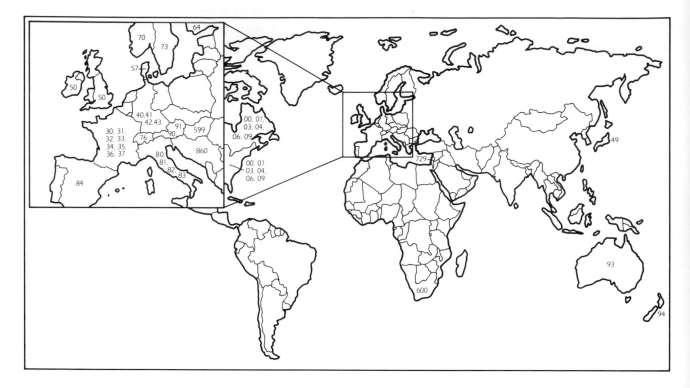

Fig. 1.47

The UK is marked 50 and any article number that is issued within
the UK begins with these particular digits. Countries where no
number is marked do not issue article numbers.

On Canadian and American bar
codes the first digit appears at the
side of the code and not along the
bottom with the other digits of the
article number. An American
bar code is shown in Fig. 1.48.

Fig. 1.48

The majority of goods are barcoded in the country of origin, with the
initial digits indicating the country in which the goods are registered.
When a multinational company is involved, however, goods may be
made in one country and registered in another.

The initial digits for periodicals and books do not depend on their
country of origin. For periodicals they are always 977, and for books
978 or 979.

EXERCISES

1. *Name three countries outside Europe that do not issue article numbers.*

2. *Which countries within Europe do not issue article numbers?*

3. *What are the country codes for Japan and Israel?*

4. *Suggest some possible reasons why some countries do not print bar codes.*

USING BAR CODES

In the stores operating computerised checkouts the bar code is
scanned by a low-power laser beam or electric light pen. This is
linked to a computer that holds the price of every article held within
the store and displays the name of the product and its price at the
till. This information is then printed on the till receipt. (The bar code
does not contain information about the product such as price, colour
or flavour.)

Fig. 1.49 illustrates
how an electronic
network for business
communication based
upon the article
numbering system
can be organised. It
represents just one
example of a number
of possible electronic
links between
companies.

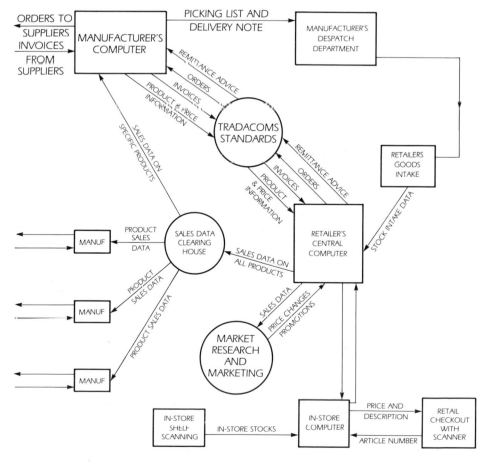

Fig. 1.49

Project Network

What is a **project**? It is clearly defined in BS 4335 as 'an enterprise involving a number of interrelated activities' and an activity is defined as 'an operation or process consuming time and possibly other resources'. (See p. 72 for an explanation of BS)

Any project, from hitching up a trailer and a car, to the launch and return of a space shuttle, requires planning. The planning may be purely a mental exercise but this can be an unsatisfactory course to follow as the project becomes more and more involved.

There are two systems that are present in any project:

• operating systems involving design, development, construction and testing; and
• management systems, which are required to plan and control the operating systems.

Project network techniques (PNT) are a group of techniques required for the description, analysis, planning and control of projects. They take into account the logical inter-relationships of all project activities, including time, costs, resources, etc. The benefits of using PNT include a clearer definition of the scope of the project and the inter-relationship between the activities. It brings about better coordination between different organisational units within the project, which relates to the units' progress and future plans. The object of project planning is to control a project, as opposed to merely monitoring what is happening. Fig. 1.50 illustrates the various resource constraints related to a specific operation, and the logical relationships that may be established by means of a network diagram.

The first process is to identify the activities to be undertaken and an order of priority. Once this has been established the order of working is determined, and from this the dependency number is established. Referring to Fig. 1.50 it is therefore logical that the walls of the bathroom cannot be tiled until the shower has been fitted, although it would be possible to paint the bathroom at any time after the plumbing has been installed, the UPVC window has been fitted and after the shower has been sited. This illustrates an inter-relationship between activities.

Priority number	Activity	Dependency number	Estimated time in hours
1	Install fixtures	None	25
2	Install plumbing	1	37
3	Fit UPVC window	1	8
4	Fit shower unit	1	6
5	Tile walls	4	10
6	Paint installation	2, 3 and 4	12

Fig. 1.50

There are two basic network types, **activity on arrow** and **activity on node**. Whether it is better to use one system rather than the other depends upon the data given. The activity on arrow diagram tends to be more established in English-speaking countries while the European countries tend to favour the activity on node method.

ACTIVITY ON ARROW

These diagrams use the **nodes** or circles, the central points in the diagram, to represent the events and the **arrows** to represent the activities. The logical relationship of events and activities in time is depicted by the direction of the arrows. Fig. 1.51 shows an example.

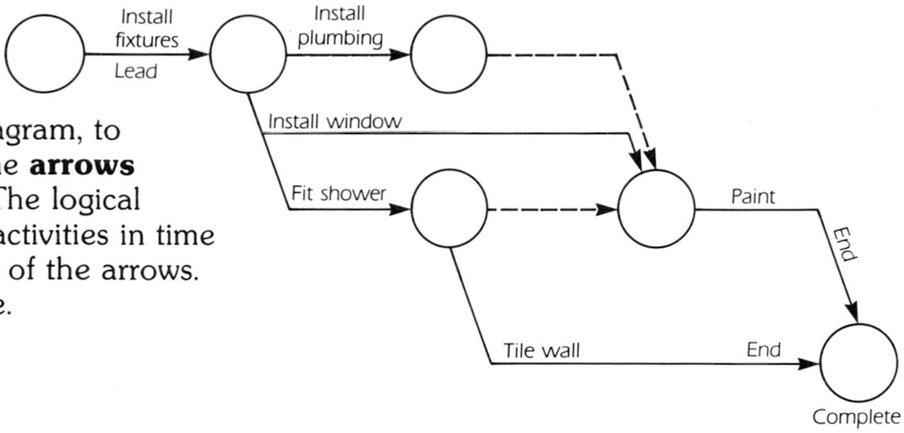

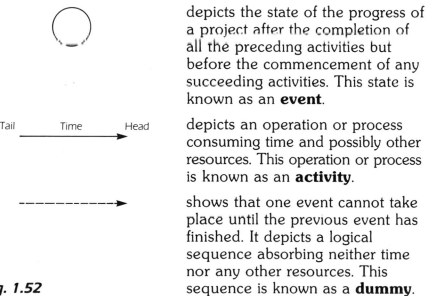

Fig. 1.51

The beginning and end of a network are identified by special activities called 'lead time' and 'end time' activities.

You will have noticed the use of three basic graphical symbols, shown again in Fig. 1.52.

depicts the state of the progress of a project after the completion of all the preceding activities but before the commencement of any succeeding activities. This state is known as an **event**.

Tail　　Time　　Head

depicts an operation or process consuming time and possibly other resources. This operation or process is known as an **activity**.

shows that one event cannot take place until the previous event has finished. It depicts a logical sequence absorbing neither time nor any other resources. This sequence is known as a **dummy**.

Fig. 1.52

ACTIVITY ON NODE

These diagrams make use of boxes instead of circles as nodes in the network as shown in Fig. 1.53 (overleaf). The nodes indicate an activity, and the arrows represent the inter-relationship and sequences of the activities.

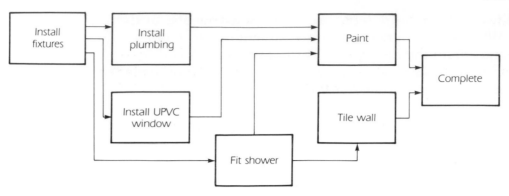

Fig. 1.53

THE CRITICAL PATH

By using activity on arrow diagrams it is possible to develop a PNT to identify the sequence of activities, and define or estimate the duration of the project and the delay for non-critical activities (known as the **float**).

This PNT is known as the **critical path method (CPM)** or **critical path analysis (CPA)** and in Fig. 1.51 the details are illustrated in a very basic form. Now study Fig. 1.54, in which the nodes have been given numbers that represent the events. Activity lines indicate the time needed for each event.

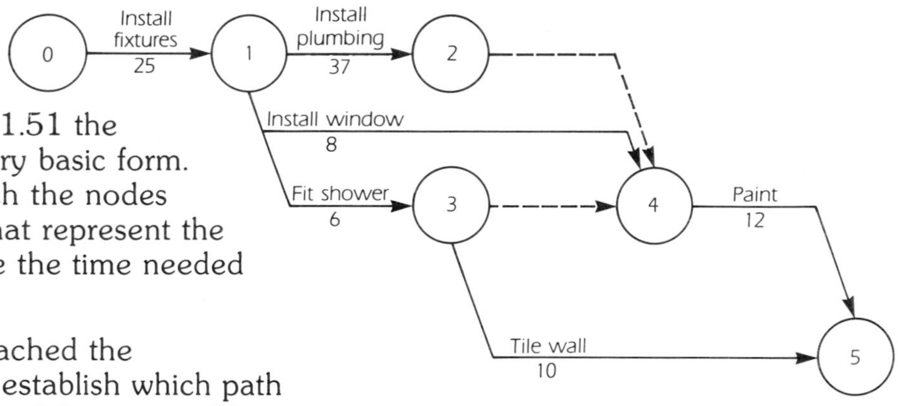

Once this stage has been reached the network can be analysed to establish which path will define the total duration of the project. You can see that the path consuming the most time (known as the critical path) has a total time of 74 hours and passes through events 1, 2, 4 and 5.

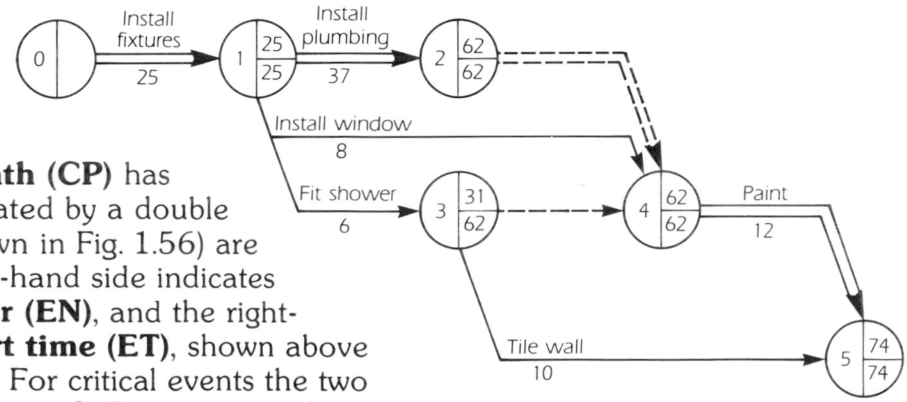

Fig. 1.54

In Fig. 1.55, the **critical path (CP)** has been identified and is indicated by a double line. The event circles (shown in Fig. 1.56) are now divided so that the left-hand side indicates the **event label** or **number (EN)**, and the right-hand side the **earliest start time (ET)**, shown above the **latest start time (LT)**. For critical events the two times are the same – the float is 0. For non-critical events the difference represents the float for that event, or the time available for the activity, in addition to its duration.

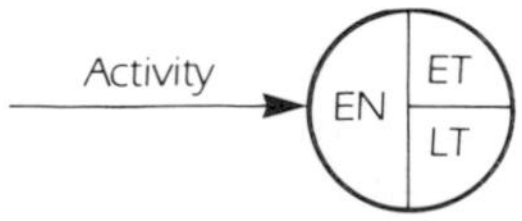

Fig. 1.55

Fig. 1.56

EXAMPLE

Fig. 1.57 shows a draft network for a small extension to an office.
The department responsible for personnel has been asked to present
to the management a network plan for the construction time so that
costings can commence.
The factors influencing the construction of the extension are as
follows.

a)	Foundations	3 days
b)	Block work to DPC	2 days
c)	Fixing windows	1 day
d)	Block work to eaves	5 days
e)	Ground floor	1 day
f)	Roof	3 days
g)	Opening up extension wall	1 day
h)	Partitions	2 days
i)	Plumber's first fix	1 day
j)	Electrician's first fix	2 days
k)	Glazing	1 day
l)	Plastering	2 days
m)	Plumber's second fix	1 day
n)	Electrician's second fix	1 day
o)	Joinery fitting	2 days
p)	Installing drainage	3 days
q)	Paving	3 days
r)	Painting	4 days
s)	Cleaning site	2 days

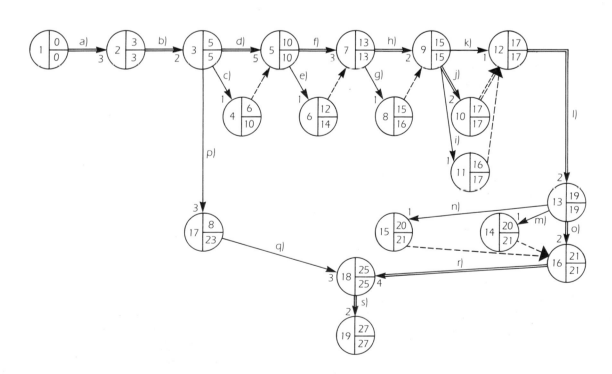

Fig. 1.57

Each possible path is listed and the CP is seen to be the route 2, 3, 5, 7, 9, 10, 12, 13, 16, 18 and 19. Fig. 1.58 shows that there is a great difference between the paths, in that the route for the quickest sequence of activities (2, 3, 17, 18 and 19) totals 13 days. This highlights that there are 14 spare days in the sequence when machines and labour could be used on another project.

Path   **Time in days**

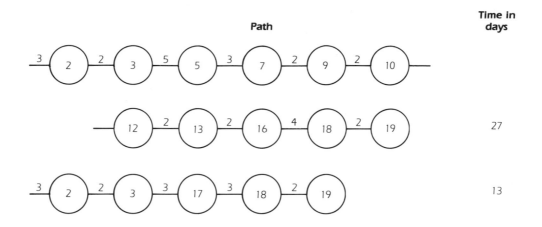

27

13

Fig. 1.58

Note that certain events have the same time for the ET and LT. These events are on the CP of the network. Any delay in completing the activities on the CP will lengthen the time taken for the overall project unless the time for subsequent events can be shortened to compensate. Activities not on the CP will have some spare time or float.

EXERCISES

1. Construct a simple project network diagram setting out the following information.
    a) Jobs B and C cannot start until job A is completed.
    b) Jobs D and E cannot start until job B is completed.
    c) Job F cannot start until jobs C and E are completed.
    d) Job G cannot start until jobs D and F are completed.

2. A motorway is being constructed at Colnbrook and a new elevated approach has to be built to give vehicles access to the motorway, near the flyover. An adequate labour force is readily available to enable work at any stage of the construction to progress.
    If you study Fig. 1.59 and the list of activities on the opposite page, it is clear why the total time necessary for these activities is estimated as 94 days. Through the development of a network, however, it will become evident where some activities can be undertaken at the same time.
    Complete a project network showing the CP and state the shortest time in which the construction project can be completed.

Activities	**Days**
a) Construct a new road to the motorway, near the flyover.	40.0
b) Close half of the old road and erect traffic lights in part A.	0.5
c) Connect new gullies (roadside drains) to the existing gullies in part A.	15.0
d) Build up the new road connection in part B.	8.0
e) Close the old road and erect traffic lights on the new road in part B.	0.5
f) Open the new road connection in part B.	0.5
g) Build up part C of the new road.	8.0
h) Remove old street lighting along the old road.	4.0
i) Remove the traffic lights on part A.	0.5
j) Remove old road between positions WX and YZ.	7.0
k) Clear and tidy the site.	10.0

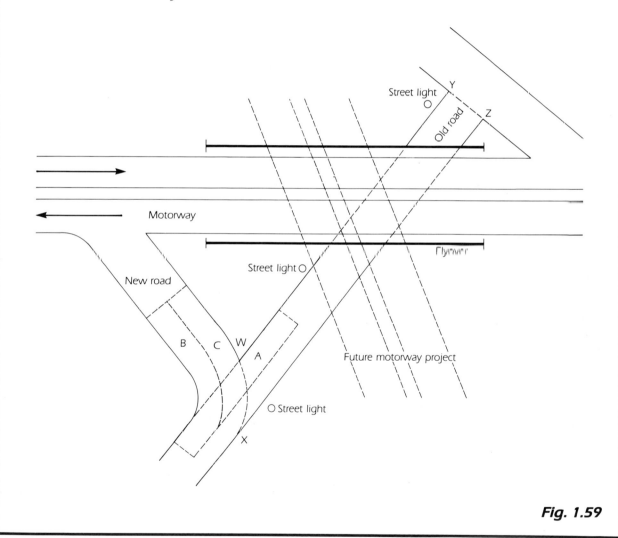

Fig. 1.59

Surface Representation

There are many situations in which we need to describe a surface by means of a diagram. A surveyor uses a survey to describe a location, for example prior to building. A map employs graphics to show the location of roads, rivers, buildings and other features. With contours it can even show the height and slope of the land.

When undertaking a journey, the motorist or pedestrian can experience only a small part of the complete journey at one time. Here we consider the use of road signs, which give information and direction so that the journey can be completed safely and efficiently.

Surveying Graphics

In order to identify areas and structures, it is essential to establish precise locations so that accurate maps and plans can be produced. To do this accurately, fully trained persons are sent out into the field and, using suitable methods, establish details that can be transposed on to maps, plans and charts.

A **field book** is the book in which a surveyor makes notes of measurements and facts that are needed for determining the boundaries, size, position, shape and area of a structure. From these sketchy but precise notes a survey plan is then drawn. Specific conventions are adhered to, as shown in Fig. 2.1.

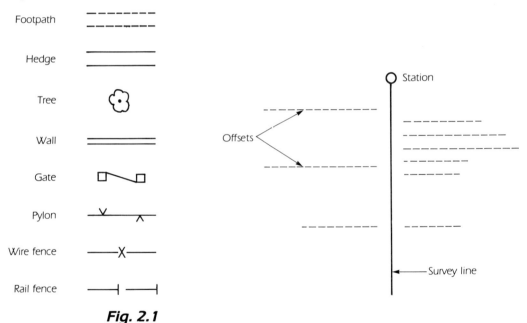

Fig. 2.1	**Fig. 2.2**

SURVEY LINES WITH OFFSETS

A chain survey line with offsets is a basic technique used when making a survey. Distances are measured to significant points (such as pylons, fences, trees, corners of buildings, etc.) which are called **stations** using a **surveyor's chain**, and from these points **offsets** are measured at 90° to the line. (See Fig. 2.2.) All the survey lines are selected to ensure an accurate coverage of all the site.

A sketch of the survey line and offsets and all the measurements taken are recorded in the field book. Two lines are drawn down the field book to represent each survey line with the datum (starting point) at the bottom of the page, marked 0 m. The offset positions are then measured and jotted down between the lines and the offset distances noted accordingly. Fig. 2.3 illustrates this, with the boundary of the site on the right and on the left a wire fence, a gate and an electric pylon.

Where the site being surveyed has a curving boundary then more offsets are required in order to plot the curve accurately.

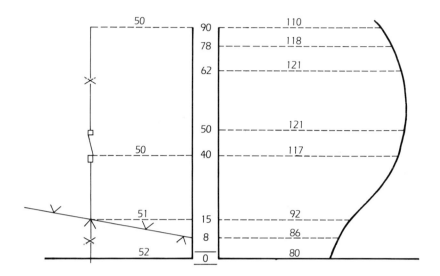

Fig. 2.3

TRIANGULATION

When an area has to be surveyed the survey lines are chosen to form a triangle, and further triangles are laid out to cover the entire area as is considered necessary. This method of surveying is called **triangulation**, and on an Ordnance Survey map a **reference station** for the purpose of triangulation is shown by the following symbol:

In Fig. 2.4 (overleaf) four stations have been used, lettered A, B, C and D. They form two triangles, ABC and ACD. Only one diagonal, AC, is required to make the triangles – diagonal DB is used for the purpose of checking, as shown in Fig. 2.5 (overleaf). These figures illustrate the field notes that would be made when surveying this particular site. (All measurements are in metres.)

It is common practice to indicate North on at least one of the sketches in the field book as it must be shown on the final survey plan.

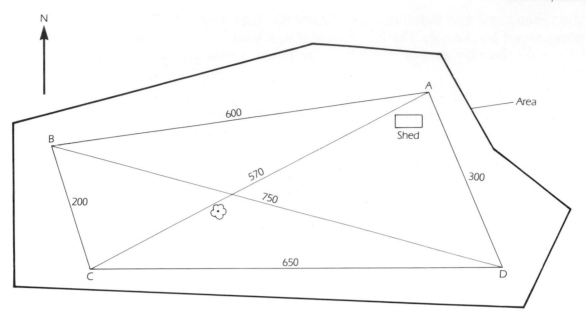

Fig. 2.4

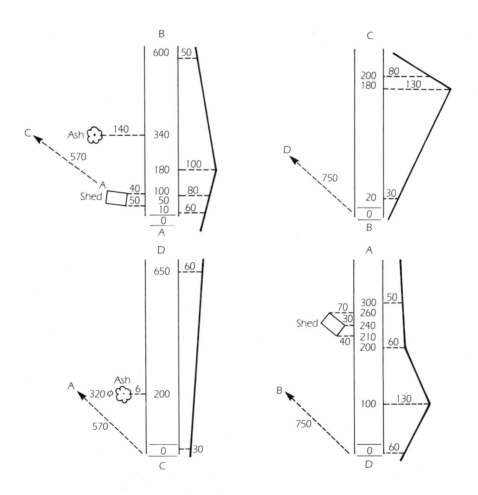

Fig. 2.5

EXERCISES

From the field notes draw the survey to a scale of 1:2500 (10 mm represents 25 m).
Mark the North indicator.
Using a tracing paper grid find the area of the site in hectares. More information
about scales and areas is given in the following paragraphs.

Supplementary information

The following scales are those that are generally recommended for use when
surveying and site plan drawing.

> *1:1250   (10 mm represents 12.5 m)*
> *1:2500   (10 mm represents 25 m)*
> *1:25 000 (10 mm represents 250 m)*
> *1:50 000 (10 mm represents 500 m)*

One hectare (ha) equals 10 000 m², i.e. a square having sides of 100 m. As a general
guide, one acre is approximately 0.4 ha, and one hectare is approximately 2.5 acres.

EXAMPLE

Find the area shown in Fig. 2.6, which has been drawn to a scale of
1:2500. The site plan has been divided into 10 mm squares; therefore
the 10 mm side of a square represents $10 \times 2500 = 25\,000$ mm,
which in turn equals 25 m.

27 squares, which were at least half covered by the shape to be
measured, were counted. 27 squares represents

$$27 \times 25\,\text{m} \times 25\,\text{m} = 27 \times 625\,\text{m}^2 = 16\,875\,\text{m}^3$$

$$= 1.688\,\text{ha}$$

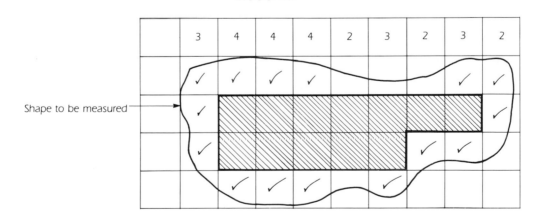

Fig. 2.6

TRAVERSE SURVEYS

On many occasions it is not possible to take diagonals across the
area that is being surveyed, for instance if there is a building in the
way, and therefore the survey lines cannot be triangulated. When
this occurs the survey lines are taken around the outside of the area

and checked by angular measurement. This method of survey is called a **traverse survey**. A **traverse** is a line of survey plotted with chained or paced distances between 90° points.

EXAMPLE

A plan is required for the house shown in outline in Fig. 2.7. A **traverse** ABCD is made by laying down a base line AB and then using a **plane table** (which is basically a protractor positioned upon a table). The lines AD, BC and DC are laid off at 90° to each other. The angle at C should then be 90° too.

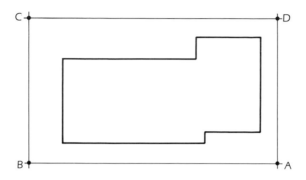

Fig. 2.7

Fig. 2.8 illustrates the entries that would appear in the field book for the survey of the house. (All the measurements are given in metres.)

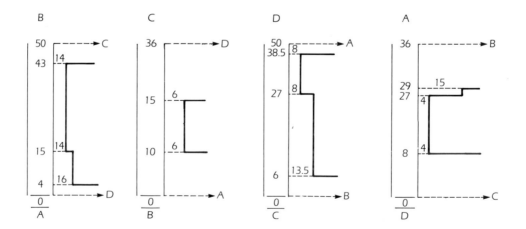

Fig. 2.8

All traverse surveys may be checked by adding up the number of degrees in all the angles of the area surveyed. A closed traverse by definition should form a polygon, because the end of the last line of the traverse should coincide with the beginning of the first line. The degrees in the angles of any polygon add up to a fixed number dependent upon the number of sides, not the length of the sides or the shape, of the polygon. The total number of degrees is given by the formula

number of degrees $= (2n - 4) \times 90°$

where *n* is the number of sides, and the external angles are measured.

EXAMPLE

In a five-sided figure:

$$(2n - 4) \times 90° = [(2 \times 5) - 4] \times 90°$$
$$= (10 - 4) \times 90°$$
$$= 540°$$

The checking and adjustment of traverse surveys

Checking of the traverse may be carried out graphically or by calculation and any **closing error** (minor error such as being a minute of a degree out) should be distributed as evenly as possible throughout the survey by a process known as **balancing** the survey.

The following graphical methods are employed where adjustment of the plan only is required and precise values of the coordinates of the stations are not required.

EXAMPLE

In Fig. 2.9 ABCDEA′ is a closed traverse which has been plotted to scale from the field measurement of lengths and included angles. A′, the last point of the traverse, does not coincide with A, the distance A′A being the closing error. Join A′A and draw lines through B,C,D and E parallel to A′A. Distances Bb, Cc, Dd and Ee are then set out on these lines proportionate to the distances of B, C, D and E respectively from the origin A of the survey. For instance, Cc equals

$$(AB + BC) \div (AB + BC + CD + DE + EA') \times A'A.$$

The adjusted traverse is then AbcdeA′.

Instead of calculating the proportionate distances as above, the process may be worked graphically, as shown in Fig. 2.10. Set out to any convenient scale a straight line ABCDEA′ such that AB, BC, CD, DE, and EA′ represent the lengths of the sides of the traverse. From A′ draw A′A″ parallel and equal to the closing error, and join AA″. Through B, C, D and E draw lines parallel to A′A″, to meet AA″ in b,c,d and e respectively. Then Bb, Cc, Dd, and Ee are the required distances.

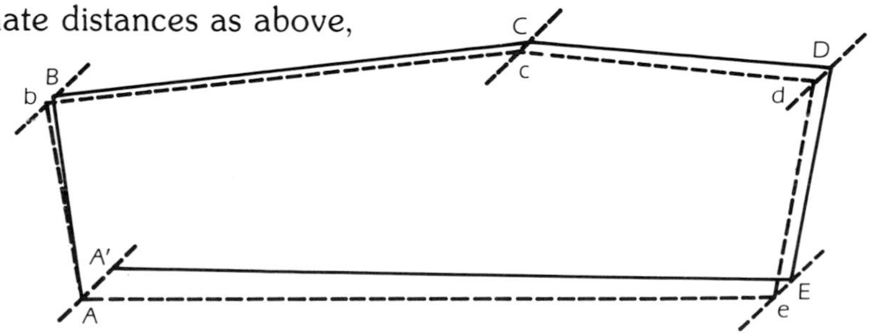

Fig. 2.9

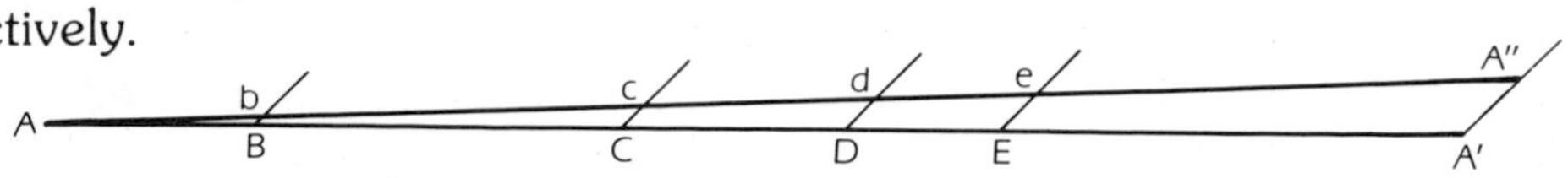

Fig. 2.10

EXERCISES

1. *Make a survey of the Craft, Design and Technology block in your school or college.*

2. *Survey the car park at your school or college in relation to the buildings.*

3. *Make a detailed survey of the school or college playing fields and include the siting of the athletics facilities that are provided.*

4. *Find the third side c of a triangle ABC in which a measures 54.8 m, b measures 42.7 m and the angle at A equals 45°.*

5. *A and B are points at the opposite ends of a lake. From a third point C measurements are made giving BC as 738 m, AC as 500 m and the angle at C as 54°.*
   Find the distance AB and the length of the lake in metres.

6. *A buoy to mark a sandbank is moored at sea opposite to and 1980 m from an observation post A on the shore. The movement of the sand bank necessitates the moving of the buoy to a new position 90° from the line of observation. From A, an angle of 11° is read to the new position of the marker buoy.*
   Find the distance in metres that the buoy is moved and the distance from A to the buoy's new position.

7. *From the central point of a railway curve, which forms part of a circle, it is found that the chord on either side measures 100 m and that the angle included by the chords is 175°.*
   Find the radius of the curve.
   N.B. The perpendicular bisector of a chord passes through the centre of the circle.

8. *Fig. 2.11 shows five pages of a field book giving the details of a chain survey. All the measurements are given in metres, to a scale of 1:1000.*
   Draw the surveyed area, starting from the point A.

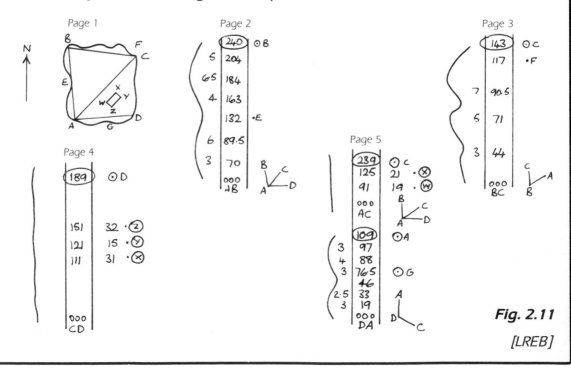

Fig. 2.11

[LREB]

Contours

The first one-inch map was published in 1801 and covered the county of Kent. During the following seven years the map was extended to cover the remainder of the country. It was initially produced in black and white and continued to be so until the end of the century when colour was first introduced. Today Ordnance Survey maps use six colours.

In the examples given on pp. 44–6 of surveying, it was taken for granted that all the initial surveying was carried out on level ground. A land survey is a two-dimensional plan of a three-dimensional site and so the distances on the map show the projected distances only in plan. These are not the true distances on the land or the true distance that one would have to travel from A to B, unless the land is perfectly flat. For example, the distance between the peaks of two mountains on a map is totally different from the actual distance one would have to travel from the peak of one down into the valley and up the second mountain to its peak.

On a map the varying heights are shown by **contour lines**. On both 1:25 000 and 1:50 000 series Ordnance Survey maps they are spaced at 10 m vertical intervals, and join all points of equal height, given to the nearest metre above sea level. They can be considered as horizontal sections through the land formation. The closer the lines are together the steeper the fall of the land.

EXAMPLE

Fig. 2.12 shows a vertical section of a land formation, and the same formation in contour lines. When a height has been surveyed a marker is usually positioned, generally in the form of a broad arrow on a stone pillar or a metal place, called a **bench mark**. (See Fig. 2.13.)

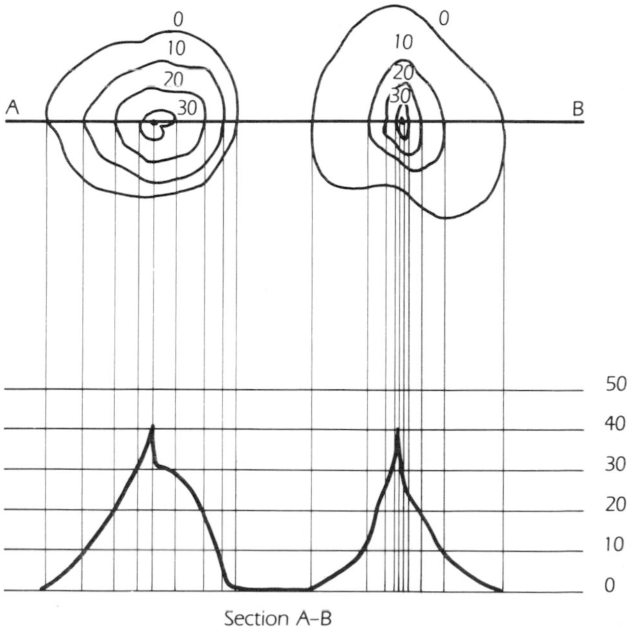

Section A-B

Fig. 2.12

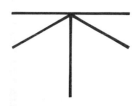

Fig. 2.13

EXERCISES

1.   Draw the section of the contour map in Fig. 2.14.

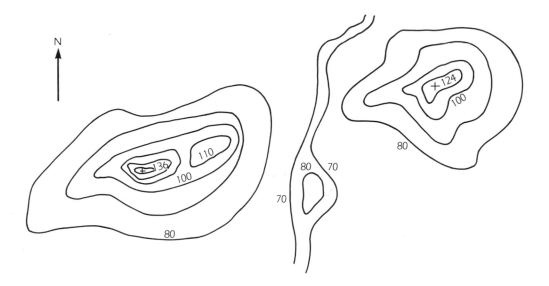

Fig. 2.14

2.   Take an Ordnance Survey map of your region. Select an area near to your home and make a sectional drawing to illustrate the contour of the land.

3.   A survey of a riverside area taken from two trees X and Y was taken. Oak trees were along the nearside river bank at points A, B, C, D, and E. Bearings taken from North are as follows:

         XA equals 6°
         XB equals 16°
         XC equals 40°
         XE equals 70°
         YD equals 14°
         YE equals 46°

     Draw a plan of the area based upon the positions of trees X and Y, where

         XA measures 25 m
         XB measures 30 m
         XC measures 45 m
         YB measures 49 m
         YD measures 34 m
         YE measures 40 m
         YC measures 39 m

     What are the lengths of YA, XD and XE?

Ordnance Survey Maps

Figs 2.15 and 2.16 (overleaf) show the symbols used on the 1:50 000 Ordnance Survey Series.

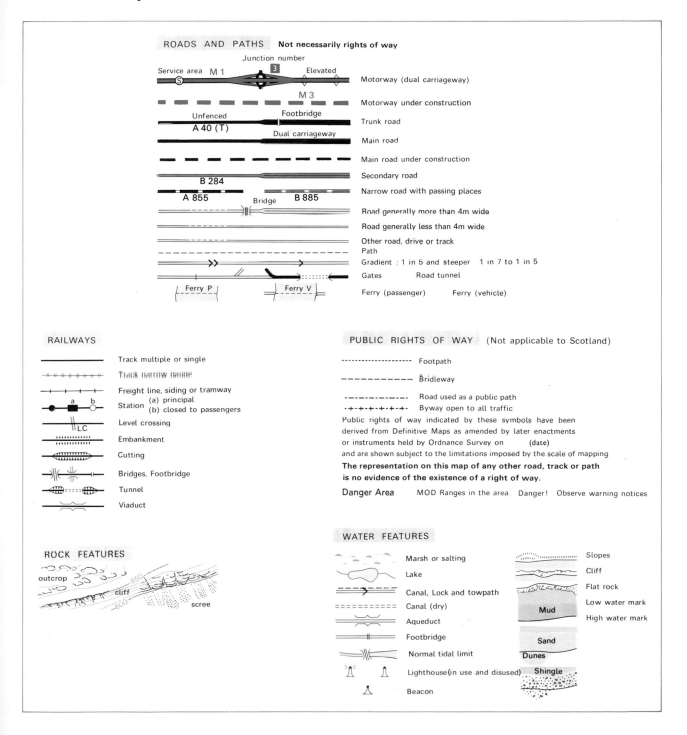

Fig. 2.15

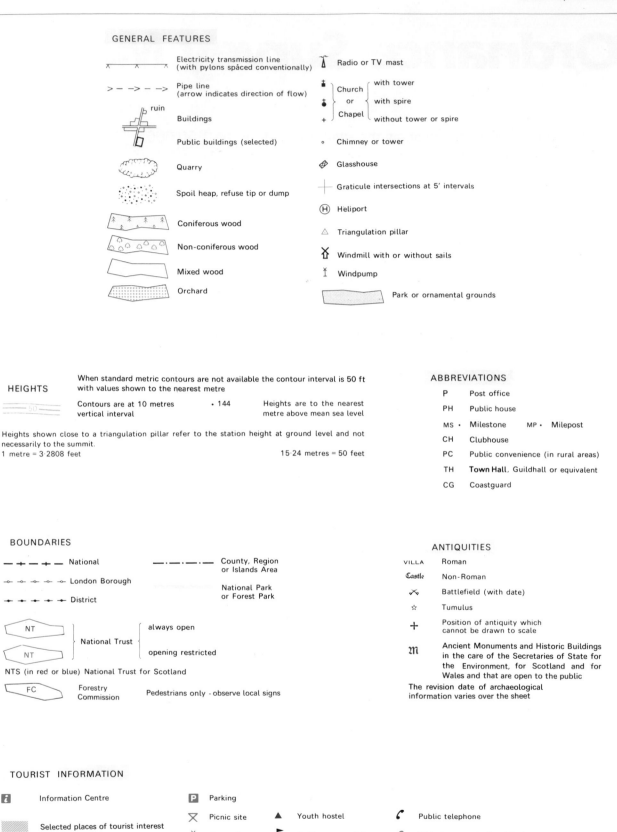

GENERAL FEATURES

Electricity transmission line
(with pylons spaced conventionally)

Radio or TV mast

Pipe line
(arrow indicates direction of flow)

Church
or
Chapel
with tower
with spire
without tower or spire

ruin

Buildings

Chimney or tower

Public buildings (selected)

Glasshouse

Quarry

Graticule intersections at 5' intervals

Spoil heap, refuse tip or dump

Heliport

Coniferous wood

Triangulation pillar

Non-coniferous wood

Windmill with or without sails

Mixed wood

Windpump

Orchard

Park or ornamental grounds

HEIGHTS

When standard metric contours are not available the contour interval is 50 ft
with values shown to the nearest metre

Contours are at 10 metres
vertical interval

• 144   Heights are to the nearest
metre above mean sea level

Heights shown close to a triangulation pillar refer to the station height at ground level and not
necessarily to the summit.
1 metre = 3·2808 feet

15·24 metres = 50 feet

ABBREVIATIONS

P   Post office

PH   Public house

MS •   Milestone   MP • Milepost

CH   Clubhouse

PC   Public convenience (in rural areas)

TH   **Town Hall**, Guildhall or equivalent

CG   Coastguard

BOUNDARIES

National

County, Region
or Islands Area

London Borough

National Park
or Forest Park

District

National Trust
always open

opening restricted

NTS (in red or blue) National Trust for Scotland

FC   Forestry
Commission

Pedestrians only - observe local signs

ANTIQUITIES

VILLA   Roman

Castle   Non-Roman

Battlefield (with date)

Tumulus

Position of antiquity which
cannot be drawn to scale

m   Ancient Monuments and Historic Buildings
in the care of the Secretaries of State for
the Environment, for Scotland and for
Wales and that are open to the public

The revision date of archaeological
information varies over the sheet

TOURIST INFORMATION

Information Centre

Parking

Public telephone

Selected places of tourist interest

Picnic site

Youth hostel

Motoring organisation telephone

Camp site

Golf course or links

Viewpoint

Caravan site

Bus or coach station

PC   Public convenience (in rural areas)

Fig. 2.16

Fig. 2.17 shows the symbols used on the 1:25 000 Ordnance Survey series.

ROADS AND PATHS   **Not necessarily rights of way**

M 1 or A 6(M)	Motorway
A 31(T)	Trunk or Main road
B 3074	Secondary road
A 35	Dual carriageway
	Gradient: 20% (1 in 5) and steeper; 14% (1 in 7) to 20% (1 in 5)
	Road generally more than 4m wide
	Road generally less than 4m wide
	Other road, drive or track

Unfenced roads and tracks are shown by pecked lines

. . . .   Path

PUBLIC RIGHTS OF WAY   (Not applicable to Scotland)
Public rights of way shown on this map may not be evident on the ground

- - - - - - - - - - } Public paths { Footpath
— — — — — — }   Bridleway
+ + + + + +   Byway open to all traffic
- + - + - + -   Road used as a public path

Information not available in uncoloured areas

DANGER AREA —
MOD ranges in the area
Danger!
Observe warning notices

Public rights of way indicated by these symbols have been derived from Definitive Maps as amended by later enactments or instruments held by Ordnance Survey

The representation on this map of any other road, track or path is no evidence of the existence of a right of way

RAILWAYS

	Multiple track } Standard gauge
	Single track
	Siding
	Narrow gauge
	Tunnel; Cutting; Embankment
	Road over; Road under; Level crossing

BOUNDARIES   As notified to March 1986

— — — —	County (England and Wales)
— — — — —	Region or Islands Area (Scotland) District
-o- -o- -o-	London Borough
. . . .	Civil Parish (England), Community (Wales)
— — — — — —	Constituency (County, Borough, Burgh or European Assembly)

SYMBOLS

Church or chapel	with tower / with spire / without tower or spire
	Lighthouse; beacon
	Building; chimney
△	Triangulation station (when coincident with symbols above shown by dot only)
	Bus or coach station
⊠ △	Glasshouse; youth hostel
· T, A, R	Telephone, public, AA, RAC
	Sloping masonry
pylon pole	Electricity transmission line

W, Spr	Well, Spring
	Site of antiquity
✕ 1066	Site of battle (with date)
	Gravel pit / Sand pit
	Other pit or quarry / Refuse or slag heap
	Loose rock / Boulders
	Outcrop / Scree
	Cliff

	Water		Mud
	Sand, sand & shingle		
	National Park or Forest Park Boundary		
NT	National Trust always open		
NT	National Trust opening restricted		
NTS NTS	National Trust for Scotland		
FC	Forestry Commission		

VEGETATION   Limits of vegetation are defined by positioning of the symbols but may be delineated also by pecks or dots

	Coniferous trees
	Non-coniferous trees
	Coppice
	Orchard

	Scrub
	Bracken, rough grassland
	In some areas bracken (a) and rough grassland (. . .) are shown separately
	Heath

Shown collectively as rough grassland on some sheets

	Reeds
	Marsh
	Saltings

HEIGHTS

50 · } Determined { ground survey
285 · } by   { air survey

Surface heights are to the nearest metre above mean sea level. Heights shown close to a triangulation pillar refer to the station height at ground level and not necessarily to the summit

75	Contours are at
60	5 metres
50	vertical interval

Fig. 2.17

EXERCISES

1. *An aerial view of a town is shown in the sketch in Fig. 2.18. On a copy of the grid in Fig. 2.19:*
    a) *complete the map using the appropriate symbols from the given list, and*
    b) *line in the shortest route to the school from the railway station.*

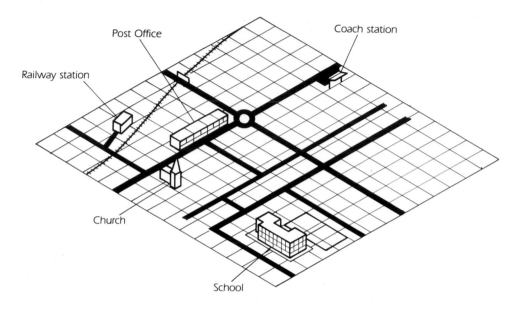

Fig. 2.18

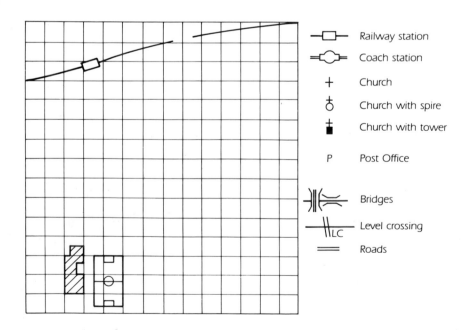

Fig. 2.19

[AEB, 1984]

2. *Study the symbols that are used on the 1:25 000 Ordnance Survey maps and convert the drawing in Fig. 2.20 into a map. Assume that there are no gradients to become involved with. The scale of Fig. 2.20 is 1:25 000.*

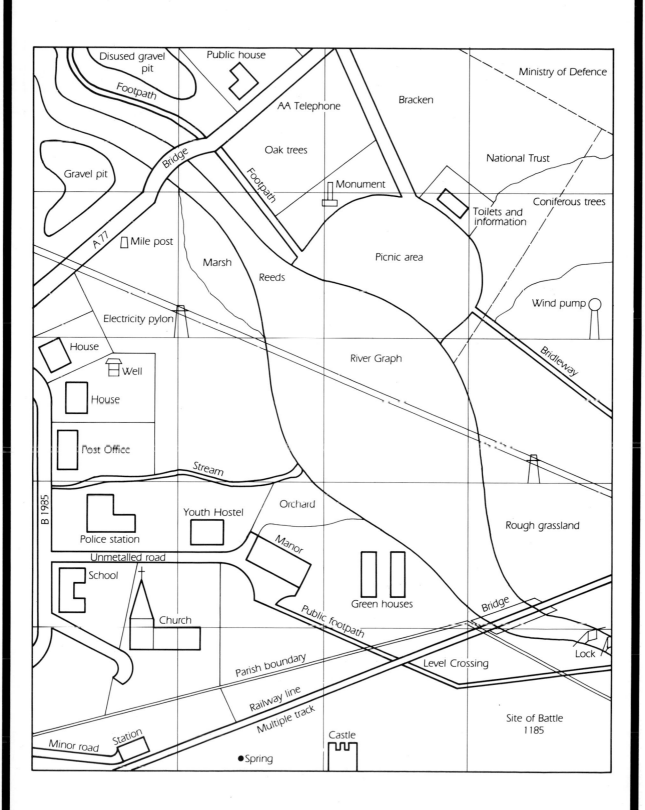

Fig. 2.20

3.   *The KP Superstore is constructing a new 'cash and save' hypermarket outside Langton Green at the position indicated by an arrow on the Ordnance Survey map in Fig. 2.21. The map is to be printed on a card and distributed to all householders in the area.*

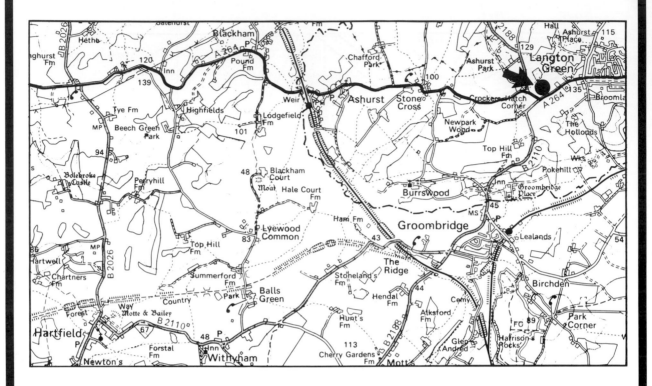

Fig. 2.21

Using information derived from the map, produce design sketches for a simplified route map that will clearly show the way to the new store from the following towns and villages: Withyham, Hartfield, Groombridge and Blackham.

Also, within an area of 160 mm × 120 mm present your outline route map and the name of the hypermarket in a manner which will achieve maximum impact.

Road Signs

The signs given below and on the following pages are taken from the Highway Code.

TRAFFIC SIGNS

Signs giving orders

These signs are mostly circular and those with red circles are mostly prohibitive.

Plates below some signs qualify their message.

Maximum speed

National speed limit applies

Stop and Give Way

Give way to traffic on major road

Warning signs

These signs are mostly triangular.

Cross roads

Roundabout

T junction

Staggered junction

Information signs

These signs are all rectangular.

Tourist information point

Permanent reduction in available lanes, e.g. two-lane carriageway reducing to one

Temporary lane closure

Bus lane
Bus lane on road at junction ahead

Signs with blue circles but no red border

These signs are mostly compulsory.

Ahead only

Turn left ahead (right if symbol reversed)

Turn left (right if symbol reversed)

Keep left (right if symbol reversed)

Other direction signs

Direction to toilets with access for the disabled

Holiday route

Route for pedestrians

Signs on non-primary routes

These signs have black borders.

On approaches to junctions

Ring road

At the junction

Local direction signs

These signs have blue borders.

On approaches to junctions

At the junction

Tourist attraction

Signs on primary routes

These signs have green backgrounds.

At the junction

Route confirmatory sign after junction

On approaches to junctions

Ring road

Direction signs

Signs on motorways
These signs are mostly rectangular with blue backgrounds.

Start of motorway and point from which motorway regulations apply

At a junction leading directly into a motorway

Route confirmatory sign after junction

Lane control signals

White arrow – lane available to traffic facing the sign. Red crosses – lane closed to traffic facing the sign.

ROAD MARKINGS

Across the carriageway

Give way to traffic on major road

Give way to traffic from right in roundabout

Along the carriageway

Double white lines

Diagonal stripes

Lane markings

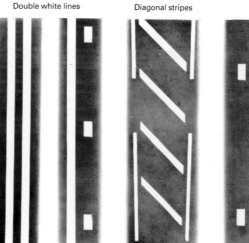

Lane line   Centre line   Hazard warning line

Zebra controlled areas

Other road markings

Keep entrance clear of stationary vehicles, even if picking up or setting down children

Warning of "Give Way" just ahead

Parking space reserved for vehicles named

Box junction

Do not block entrance to side road

Along the edge of the carriageway

Waiting restrictions
No waiting on carriageway, pavement or verge (except to load or unload or while passengers board or alight) at times shown on nearby plates or on entry signs to controlled parking zones.

If no days are indicated on the sign, the restrictions are in force every day including Sundays and Bank Holidays. The lines give a guide to the restriction in force but the time plates must be consulted.

No waiting for at least eight hours between 7 am and 7 pm on four or more days of the week

No waiting for at least eight hours between 7 am and 7 pm on four or more days of the week plus some additional period outside these times

During any other periods

Examples of plates indicating restriction times

Continuous prohibition

Plate giving times

Mon - Sat
8 am - 6 pm
Waiting limited
to 20 minutes
Return prohibited
within 40 minutes

Limited waiting

On the kerb or at edge of carriageway

Loading restrictions
No loading or unloading at times shown on nearby plates. If no days are indicated on the sign, the restrictions are in force every day including Sundays and Bank Holidays.

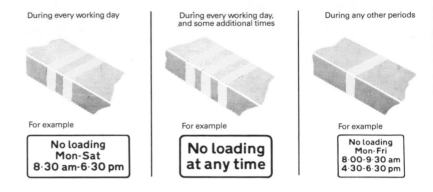

During every working day

For example

> No loading
> Mon-Sat
> 8·30 am-6·30 pm

During every working day, and some additional times

For example

> **No loading
> at any time**

During any other periods

For example

> No loading
> Mon-Fri
> 8·00-9·30 am
> 4·30-6·30 pm

RAILWAY CROSSINGS

Signs at level crossings

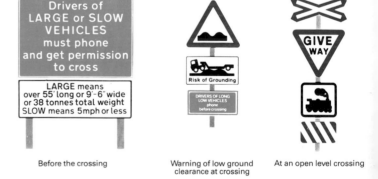

Before the crossing

Warning of low ground clearance at crossing

At an open level crossing

Automatic open crossings

Some level crossings with no gates, barriers or attendant have amber lights followed by flashing red 'STOP' lights. When the lights show you must stop and wait. Do not cross the railway – a train will reach the crossing soon after the lights begin to show. If one train has gone by, but the lights continue to flash, you must wait as another train will soon arrive. The lights will go out when it is safe to cross.

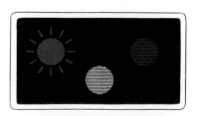

At level crossings, lifting bridges, airfields, fire stations, etc

Automatic half-barrier level crossings

These crossings have automatic barriers across the left side of the road. The trains work the barriers, which fall just before the train reaches the crossing. Amber lights and an alarm followed by flashing red 'STOP' lights warn you when the barriers are about to come down. Do not move on to the railway once these signals have started – the train cannot stop and will be at the crossing very soon. Wait at the 'STOP' line. If you are on foot, wait at the barrier, or the broken white line on the road or footpath, or by the wicket gate. Never zigzag round the barriers – you could be killed and endanger other lives. If one train has gone by, but the barriers stay down and the red lights continue to flash, you must wait as another train will soon arrive.

MOTORWAY SIGNALS

Special signals are used on motorways. In normal conditions they are blank. In dangerous conditions, amber lights flash and a panel in the middle of the signal shows either a special temporary maximum speed or which lanes are closed. When the danger has been passed the panel of the next signal will show (without flashing lights) the end of restriction signal.

On most motorways, the signals are on the central reservation at intervals of not more than two miles and they apply to all lanes. On some very busy motorways, the signals are overhead, one applying to each lane.

Some signals have red lights as well. If the red lights above your lane flash, you must not go beyond the signal in that lane. If red lights flash on a slip road, you must not enter it.

Some motorways still have flashing amber signals at the entrances and at one- or two-mile intervals. These warn of danger; for example, an accident, fog or risk of skidding. When the signals are flashing, keep your speed under 30 mph until you are sure it is safe to go faster.

Roadside signals

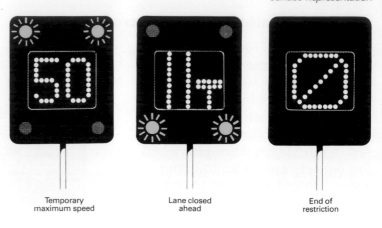

Temporary
maximum speed

Lane closed
ahead

End of
restriction

Overhead signals

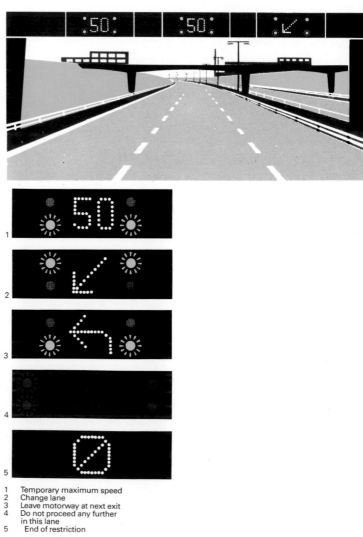

1 Temporary maximum speed
2 Change lane
3 Leave motorway at next exit
4 Do not proceed any further
  in this lane
5 End of restriction

Shortest stopping distances

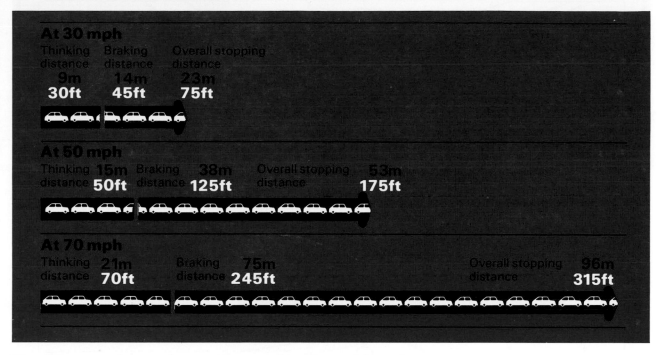

The distances shown above are in car lengths and based upon an average family saloon.

Shortest stopping distances – in feet

mph	Thinking distance	Braking distance	Overall stopping distance
20	20	20	40
30	30	45	75
40	40	80	120
50	50	125	175
60	60	180	240
70	70	245	315

On a dry road, a good car with good brakes and tyres and an alert driver will stop in the distances shown. Remember these are shortest stopping distances. Stopping distances increase greatly with wet and slippery roads, poor brakes and tyres, and tired drivers.

EXERCISES

1. *Study the road signs from the Highway Code that are given on pages 59–65, and complete the map in Fig. 2.22, where there are numbered sites for specific road signs. Several signs may be used on one site. Select the signs that match most closely the specific road conditions shown in Fig. 2.23.*
    Make a scale drawing of the map and make up a key, and then draw each of the signs appropriate to the specific conditions of the road, using colour.

←30 m→

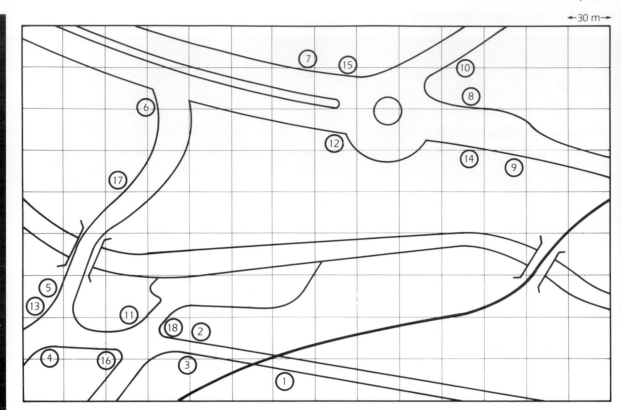

Fig. 2.22

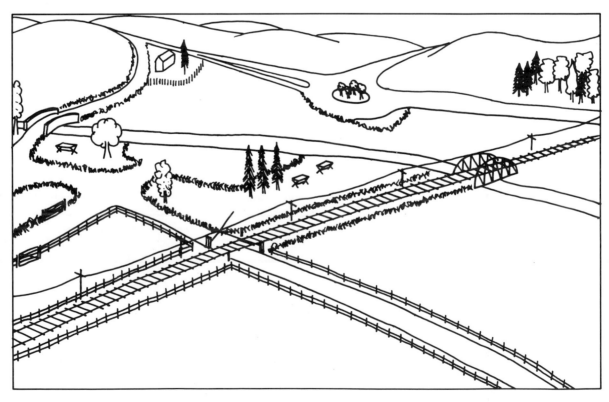

Fig. 2.23

2.   The drawing in Fig. 2.24 shows the plan of a shopping precinct with access to car parking only at the positions marked **O**.
Devise a scheme of signposting that could be erected, to include:
  a) signs for inside a car park showing the direction of flow for the cars and directions for pedestrians,
  b) signs for use outside a parking area giving relevant information, and
  c) signs within the shopping area indicating access to the different car parks.
The use of different colours, numbers and letters to help distinguish specific information should be considered. Draw a key to explain the meaning of the symbols that you use.

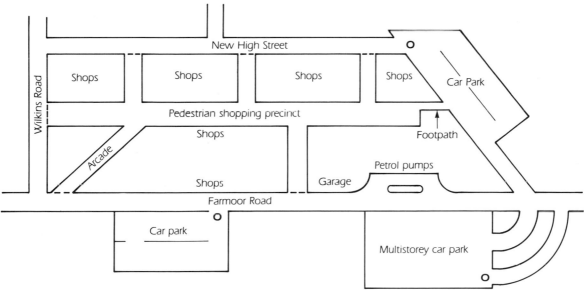

Fig. 2.24

3.   Study the map in Fig. 2.25 and write down directions for the shortest possible route to the hotel from the railway station for a taxi and for a pedestrian.

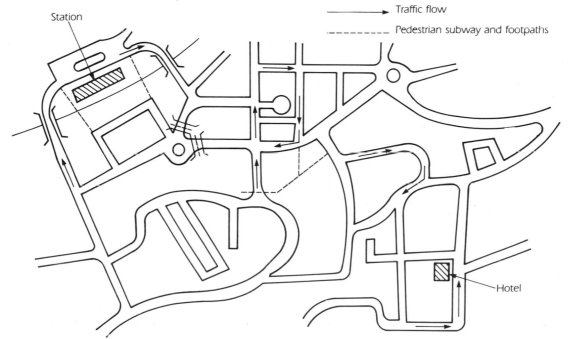

Fig. 2.25

4. *The plan in Fig. 2.26 shows the central part of a city. Indicated on it in heavy lines is the route of a new underground system, with the proposed stations. The name selected for the system after great discussion is Abra Underground.*

   a) *Design and draw, using instruments, a logo incorporating the initial letters of the underground system.*

   b) *Draw a simplified map of the underground system that would be suitable for use on public display boards, pocket folders and the inside cover of a diary. The names of the stations must be included.*

The use of colour and shading is important.

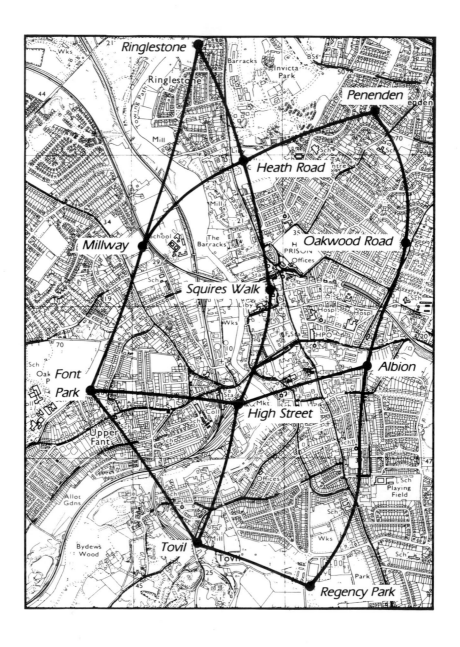

Fig. 2.26

5. *Fig. 2.27 represents an Intercity rail network.*
Calculate the journey time from Sheffield to London, and state from which London station one would depart in order to travel to Manchester.

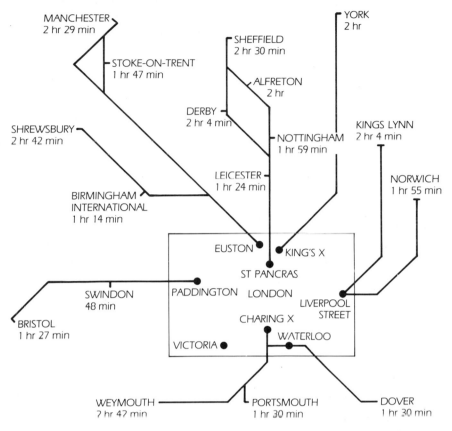

Fig. 2.27

[AEB, 1985]

Section 3

Systems

Graphics are a very effective means of expressing ideas in symbolic form to other people or to organisations. Communication becomes much more effective when everybody within a field of study adopts a **system** of graphical symbols – in effect, a language. In this section we shall study some systems in common use, particularly in the planning, building, and electrical and mechanical engineering trades.

British Standards

In 1901 the **British Standards Institution** (BSI) was formed and has developed into the national body wholly responsible for the preparation and publication of required standards. The BSI is a non-profit making organisation and is totally independent of any other body. It is financed mainly by the sale of standards and by testing and certification fees. Other contributions come from membership subscriptions from individuals, industry, and local authorities, and from an annual government grant.

British Standards are accepted as national guidelines for the world of industry and commerce. They define standards for technical criteria, economic production, safety and fitness for people. They assist in the reduction of unnecessary product variety, simplify and rationalise manufacturing processes and encourage interchangeability. They also make communication between professional people effective, since everybody can speak the same technical language.

In many areas of life we encounter articles that meet the specific standards that are governed by the British Standards Institution. These articles are granted a specific number against the letters BS, which signifies that they have been manufactured to an agreed standard.

EXERCISES

1. *Find each of the articles in the following list and write down the BS number for each, should it have been granted one:*

car number plate	13 A socket
hot-water bottle	manhole cover
13 A plug	knitting wool label

2. *Study the symbols in Fig. 3.1 and identify where they can be found. Give examples and any other informative details that could be relevant. Draw up a chart as illustrated in Fig. 3.2 to assist you in giving your answer.*

BS 857

BS 2869C1

Fig. 3.1

Symbol	Name of symbol	Where used	What it signifies
	Double insulation mark	Household appliances (electrical) e.g. vacuum cleaners, shavers, curling tongs, hair dryers, table lamps	The appliance has double insulation and/or reinforced insulation throughout. There is no provision for earthing.

Fig. 3.2

3. An **ideogram** is a symbol that attempts to convey the content of an idea easily and quickly.
   Design a car dash panel that can be internationally recognised to illustrate the following information for the driver:

   a) left indicator on

   b) right indicator on

   c) ignition on

   d) engine temperature

   e) battery charging

   f) engine oil low

   g) hazard warning light on

   h) parking lights on

   i) bonnet open

   j) boot lid open

   k) rear doors unlocked

   l) washer bottle requires refilling

   m) front disc pads require replacing

   n) rear brake shoes require replacing

   o) outside air temperature is below 0°

   p) trailer connected to car

4. When designing a symbol to illustrate a particular activity it is vitally important to keep it as simple as possible. An outline or silhouette is a good starting point, but care must be taken with regard to proportions. Ink and the use of colour will improve the visual effect, but too many colours can confuse the message.
   Design symbols to be displayed outside a sports complex that will represent the following activities:

   a) cycling

   b) rowing

   c) fencing

   d) trampolining

   e) basketball

   f) athletics

5. *How can you illustrate the following information on an aerosol can of spray paint using symbols?*

   a) Shake the container for two minutes.

   b) Spray 250 mm from the object.

   c) Keep the can moving while spraying.

   d) Invert the can and depress the nozzle after use in order to clear the nozzle.

   e) Store above 10 °C.

   f) This container is flammable.

Present your graphic information in an orderly sequence.

6. *An author is writing a cookery book of recipes for a slow cooker. Each recipe is to be headed by a set of symbols to illustrate the descriptions listed below. You have been commissioned to devise the rating symbols.*

   a) The recipe is easy to prepare..

   b) The recipe needs a little special care during part or all of its preparation.

   c) The heat settings and cooking time must not be altered.

   d) The recipe should not be prepared by the one-step method.

   e) The recipe is suitable for freezing.

   f) The recipe serves x number of people.

   g) The recipe makes an economy meal.

Domestic Water Systems

The majority of housing today is fitted out with a hot water system in which the cold water tank, the cistern, feeds water to the boiler. Hot water from the boiler heats the heating coils in the indirect cylinder, which then heat the water inside the indirect cylinder. This is then run off to the various supplies within the home. See Fig. 3.3.

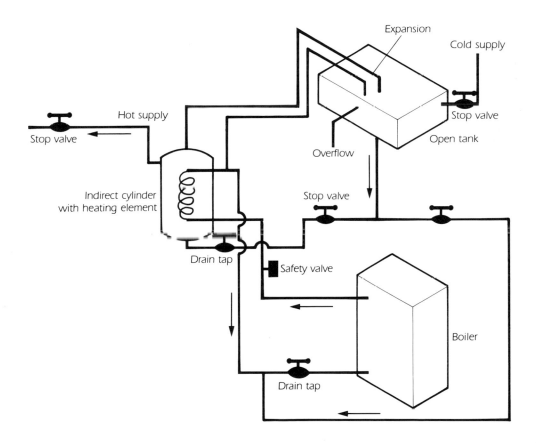

Fig. 3.3

Using the symbols given in Fig. 3.4 (overleaf), you can draw a circuit without having to draw the specific units employed within it. See Fig. 3.5 (overleaf). (For an explanation of 'BS', see p. 72.)

Add to a copy of the circuit diagram in Fig. 3.5 the water supplies to the kitchen sink and to the bath, wash basin and toilet. The dashed lines indicate feeder pipes to be connected into the system. Include supplementary fitments where you feel they would be an advantage.

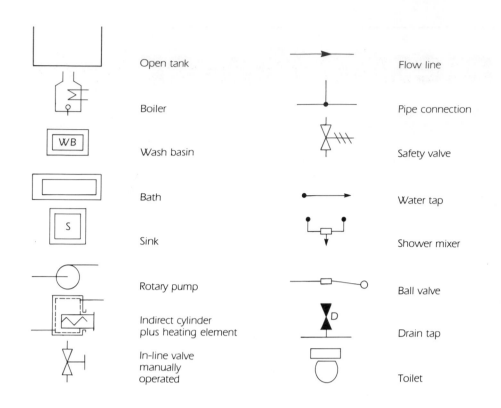

Open tank	Flow line
Boiler	Pipe connection
Wash basin	Safety valve
Bath	Water tap
Sink	Shower mixer
Rotary pump	Ball valve
Indirect cylinder plus heating element	Drain tap
In-line valve manually operated	Toilet

Fig. 3.4

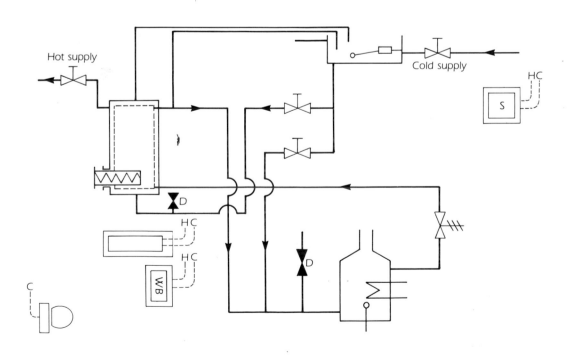

Fig. 3.5

Further Domestic Symbols

Further domestic symbols used when planning the interior and exterior layout of a property are shown in Fig. 3.6, and symbols for heating systems in Fig. 3.7. Fitments and facilities are drawn to the same scale as the plan of the environment in which they are to be sited. It is then possible, by moving the scaled-down drawings of fixtures around, to determine their ideal siting. The windows may also be drawn to scale and positioned in the best places, the apex of the broken lines indicating the hinged side of the opening light.

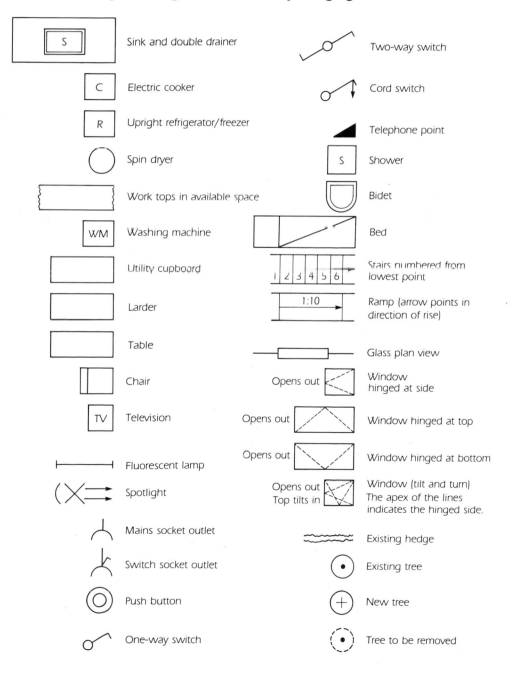

Fig. 3.6

Heating surfaces

Convectors:

Natural

Fan

Embedded panels:

Floor
face view

Ceiling
face view

Unit heaters:

Horizontal*

Downward*

*Heater: H or +
 Cooler: C or −

Radiator panel

Radiant panel:
Wall mounted

Ceiling mounted
face view

Towel rail

Fig. 3.7

EXERCISES

1. Bathroom design is extremely important today with many new styles of fitments
    now available. Try planning a new design for your bathroom at home.
    Measure your bathroom and transfer the basic dimensions on to a grid like the one
    in Fig. 3.8. Indicate the positions of the windows and doors. Make tracings of the
    bathroom fixtures (see Fig. 3.9) that you feel you would like to include in your
    redesigned suite, and establish your ideal layout. You can do this by cutting out the
    fixtures you want and putting them on the grid. Additional walls may be added
    should you feel them to be necessary.
    Indicate on your plan any recommendations for the layout of the required services.

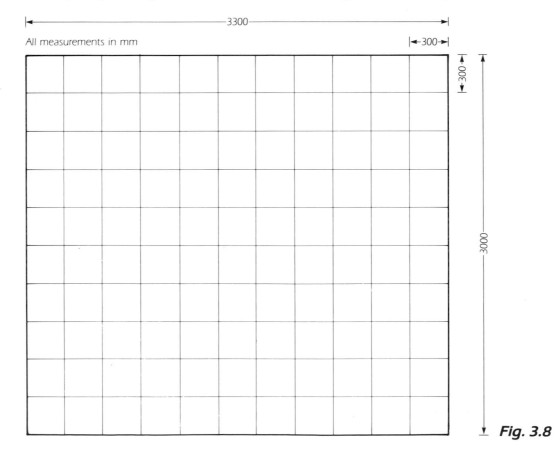

Fig. 3.8

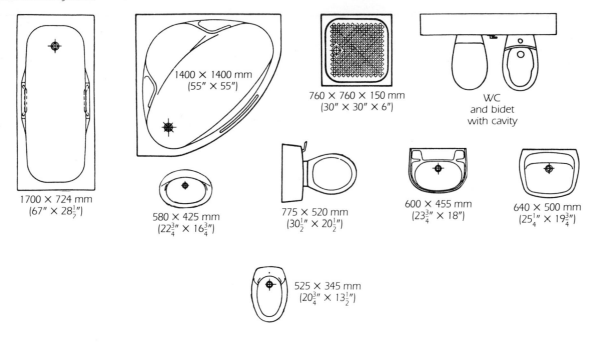

Fig. 3.9

2. *In question **1** you were requested to plan a new layout for your bathroom at home. Referring to p. 75 make a circuit diagram of your own hot water system to show your revised bathroom layout.*

3. *The diagram in Fig. 3.10 shows a control system for water supplying a basin, shower and a bath.*

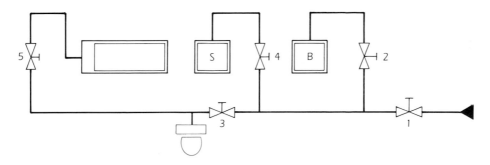

Fig. 3.10

a) Which of the valves would have to be turned off to repair a dripping bath tap but allow the basin and shower still to be used?

b) What could be repaired if valve 3 was turned off?

c) When would valve 1 be used?

Scaled Plans

Fig. 3.11 shows the types of line used in building drawing.

Continuous lines

Line thickness	Thick	Medium	Thin
Technical pen size	▬▬▬ 0.8 mm	▬▬ 0.4 mm	▬▬ 0.2 mm
Site location Block plan	Plot outline New building	Existing building	Boundaries Roads Reference grid
Site plan	Plot outline Building outline	General details Boundaries	Reference grid Dimensions Hatching
Location drawing Assembly drawings	Walls Slabs (structural)	Windows Doors etc Components in elevation	Reference grid Dimensions Hatching

Other lines

Hidden detail	‒ ‒ ‒ ‒ ‒ ‒	North point	
Centre lines 'Lines of symmetry	‒‒ ‒ ‒‒ ‒	Direction of view	→
Break line	‒‒‒╱╲╱‒‒‒	Damp proof course	▬▬ DPC ▬▬
Drain or sewer	▬ ‒ ▬ ▬ ‒ ▬	Vertical damp proof course	VDPC
Outline of adjacent parts	▬ ‒ ‒ ▬ ‒ ‒ ▬		

Fig. 3.11

Fig. 3.12 shows building materials in section (BS 1192 – see p. 72 for an explanation of BS).

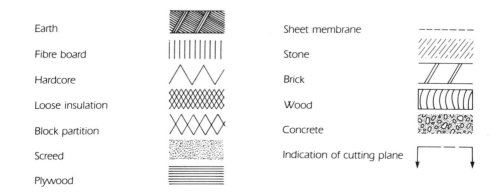

Earth		Sheet membrane	
Fibre board		Stone	
Hardcore		Brick	
Loose insulation		Wood	
Block partition		Concrete	
Screed		Indication of cutting plane	
Plywood			

Fig. 3.12

The recommended colours for indicating building materials are as follows:

Material	Colour
Cast iron	Payne's grey
Wrought iron	Prussian blue
Steel	Purple
Brass, gunmetal, phosphor bronze	Light yellow
Copper	Crimson lake
Aluminium, tin, white metals, light alloys	Light green
Brickwork	Vermilion
Concrete	Light green
Earth, rock	Sepia
Timber	Burnt sienna
Glass	Pale blue
Insulation (electrical)	Black

EXERCISES

1. *Draw the kitchen area shown in Fig. 3.13 to a convenient larger scale. Draw the appropriate domestic items to the same scale, bearing in mind that the majority of furniture produced today has a depth of 600 mm and works in length multiples of either 500 mm, 600 mm or 1000 mm. Cut out your drawings and arrange them in suitable positions in the area. When placed in a satisfactory position glue them in place.*

   The hot and cold water supply may be sited where it is convenient to your design layout. Refer to Fig. 3.6.

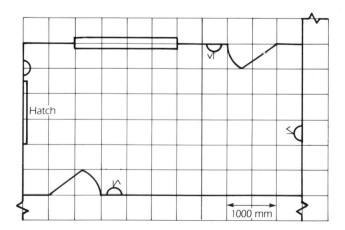

Hatch

1000 mm

Fig. 3.13

2. Draw the bedsitting room in Fig. 3.14 and add the items that you think you would require if you were living in such a situation.
The services indicated are in fixed positions and cannot be moved.

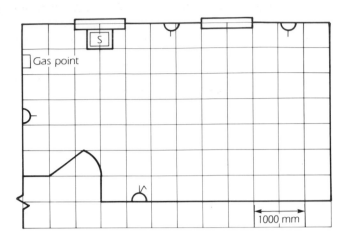

Gas point

1000 mm

Fig. 3.14

3. Figs. 3.15 and 3.16 show details of a development that is going to be built in your locality. The block plan in Fig. 3.15 shows the site layout and the location plans in Fig. 3.16 illustrate the upper and lower maisonettes in one unit.
You have been requested by the local planning authority to:
a) make a scaled drawing of one of the units illustrating the type of windows that you envisage will be installed and the type of front door that will be used throughout the site.
b) make a large scale plan of both the maisonettes and include all the relevant fixtures and fittings that you consider essential to anybody occupying the units. The scale used must be stated clearly on the drawing.
c) place representative units on both the scale drawings illustrating the requirements of anybody living in the premises, e.g. tables, chairs, bed, sink, cupboard.

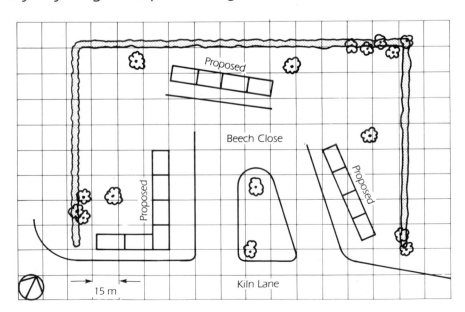

Proposed

Beech Close

Proposed

Proposed

15 m

Kiln Lane

Fig. 3.15

d) *The development has not been planned with garages or parking space for use by the occupants, and the planning authority has stated that garages have to be built somewhere on the site. You therefore have to decide upon where these garages have to be sited, and the size of the garage unit. Access is also important in order to eliminate congestion. You are therefore requested to make a scale drawing of the site and place the garages in a suitable but inconspicuous postion.*

e) *Make an impression sketch of the site and include figures and the siting of new trees. The use of colour is to be considered.*

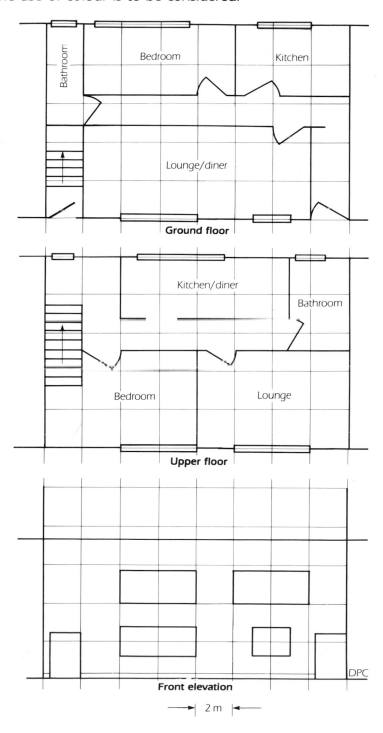

Fig. 3.16

AXONOMETRIC PROJECTION

Axonometric projection is a commonly used metric system of projection which is particularly suited to illustrating the layout of buildings, furniture, plant and equipment. The system is used by many architects, interior designers and factory planners.

The visual impression that is given by this method of projection is that of looking down on to the object from a high vantage point, with all the horizontal surfaces being drawn as in a true plan view. This is the reason that the system is often referred to as planometric.

The angles commonly employed are 30° and 60° or 45° and 45°, but it is quite permissible to use any combination of angles providing that they always add up to 90°.

Any vertical lines are always drawn in the vertical plane. All the vertical and horizontal lines are drawn full size or to scale. Inclined lines are drawn to the selected angle with inclined surfaces. For example, circles are drawn using a grid and appear as ellipses.

EXAMPLE

A simple exercise would be to draw a rectangular box with a vertical height of 70 mm, one side 100 mm long and the remaining side 60 mm long, using two angles of 45°. Now on one side of the box construct, using the grid method, a circle of diameter 50 mm. See Fig. 3.17.

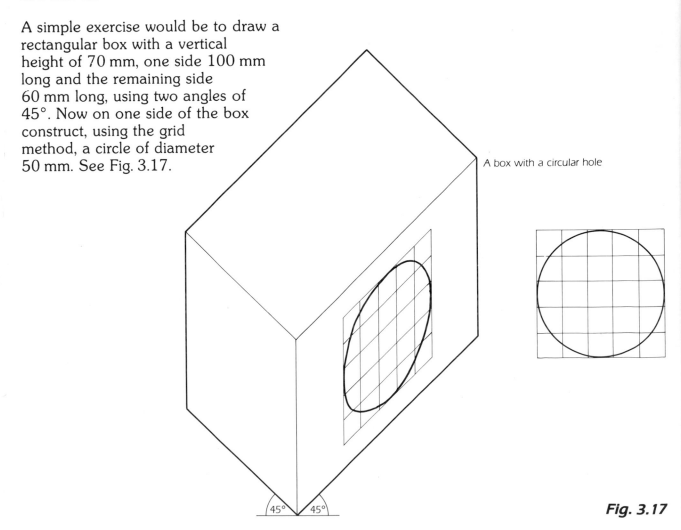

A box with a circular hole

Fig. 3.17

Now look at the interior layout of the kitchen in Fig. 3.18, which has been drawn using 30° and 60° angles. You will notice that the rectangular top surfaces of objects do not appear to be rectangular, but this is purely an optical illusion. In fact they are truly rectangular.

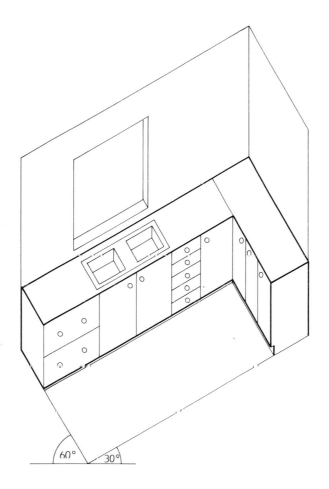

Fig. 3.18

OBLIQUE PROJECTION

Oblique projection is a useful method of portraying in only one view an object with curves or circles. It is not a true system of projection, since the drawing of the front face obscures the sides of the object which are perpendicular to the front face. This is overlooked in the interests of convenience and simplicity.

It is recommended that any view having curves is initially drawn in orthographic projection, with the side views then drawn using parallel lines at an angle of 45° to the horizontal. Should the same scale be used along the inclined parallel sides as for the front face, as in

Fig. 3.19, the projection becomes known as a **Cavalier projection**. This is not commonly used because it projects a distorted view, so in order to correct this the measurements that are projected rearwards are drawn to the generally agreed specification of half-scale. See Fig. 3.20.

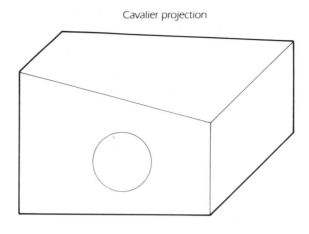

Cavalier projection

Fig. 3.19

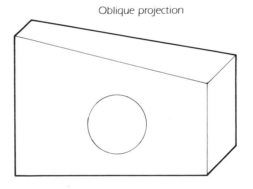

Oblique projection

Fig. 3.20

ISOMETRIC PROJECTION

Isometric projection is used in order to portray a three-dimensional object by means of only one drawing based upon the isometric axes shown in Fig. 3.21. In conventional isometric drawing the full dimensions of the object are drawn from the origin O and projected in two directions OA and OB, both set at 30° to the horizontal as shown in Fig. 3.22. This results in a view that is in effect larger than life, with no account being taken of foreshortening the sloping sides (see p. 90).

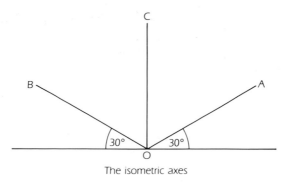

The isometric axes

Fig. 3.21

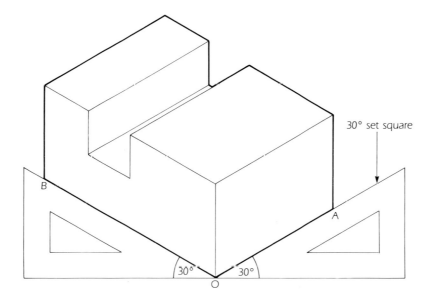

30° set square

Fig. 3.22

Fig. 3.23 shows an example of drawing a hexagonal prism in isometric projection.

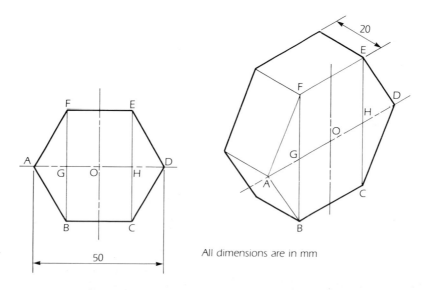

All dimensions are in mm

Fig. 3.23

EXAMPLE

Figs. 3.24 and 3.25 show how to draw a circle in isometric projection. Using a prescribed diameter of 100 mm draw a circle having a 50 mm radius. Draw the lines AB and DC at right angles to each other and passing through the centre of the circle. Using the compass set at the radius of the circle divide the circumference into twelve equal divisions and number each point. Draw the ordinates 2,12, 3,11, etc. with each ordinate passing through the line AB and at 90° to it. See Fig. 3.24.

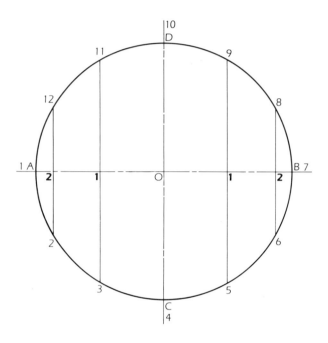

Fig. 3.24

For the isometric projection, draw a line AB set at 30° to the horizontal and passing through the centre of the position where the isometric circle (which in effect is an ellipse) has to be drawn. At position O now erect a perpendicular. With the compass set at the radius of the circle in Fig. 3.24, OA, strike arcs to determine the positions of points A,B,C and D relative to O.

With a compass set to distance O**1** on Fig. 3.24 mark the same distance out from the point O along the line AB on the isometric drawing, as in Fig. 3.25. Do likewise with distance O**2**. Taking a compass once again on Fig. 3.24, set the compass to distance **1**,11 and mark off point 11 from point **1** to the same measurement, as in Fig. 3.25. Continue this process for the other points in Fig. 3.24.

Distance O,**2** equals distance **1**,3, distance O,**1** equals distance **2**,12, and so on.

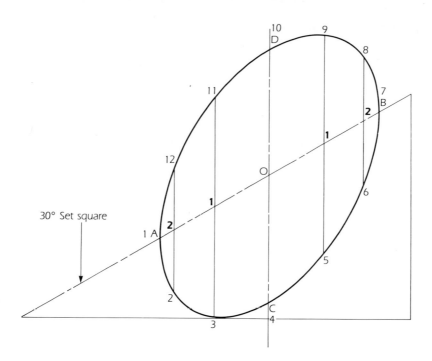

Fig. 3.25

To convert Fig. 3.25 to a drawing of a cylinder of depth 20 mm, a line PQ is drawn at 30° to AB passing through O, indicating the two extremities of the ellipse. With a 30° set square draw tangents to these two points. Progressively work around the ellipse drawing parallels at the ends of the ordinates as shown in Fig. 3.26. Set a compass to the required distance, in this case 20 mm, and mark along the 30° parallels around the ellipse.

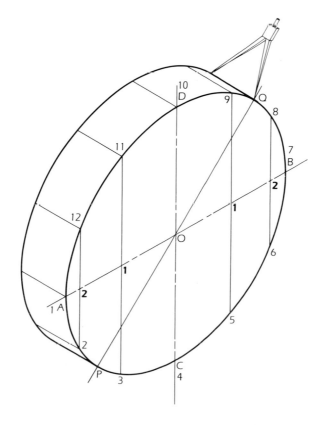

Fig. 3.26

Taking account of foreshortening

In the examples we have looked at, there has been no allowance made for the foreshortening effect that should be seen when looking at an object which is receding into the distance. For convenience the lengths that are parallel to the isometric axes are drawn full size, so the conventional isometric drawing appears larger than full size.

EXAMPLE

Make a copy of Fig. 3.27. You will notice that the true angle of tilt of the cube base, angle *a* in the side elevation, is approximately 35° The exact value of this angle is 35° 16′.

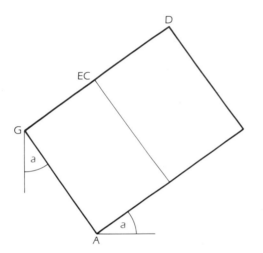
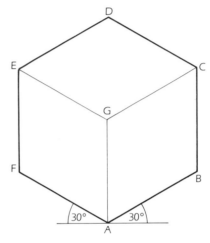

Fig. 3.27

When it is required to draw a true isometric projection, taking into account the foreshortening effect, an isometric scale has to be drawn. A line at 45° to the base line is drawn, and then from the same point on the base line another line is projected at 30°, as in Fig. 3.28. The true length of one of the sides is measured out on the line at 45° to the base line. A vertical line is projected downwards until it crosses the 30° line. This now represents the foreshortened line that has to be drawn on the isometric axes, as shown in Fig. 3.28.

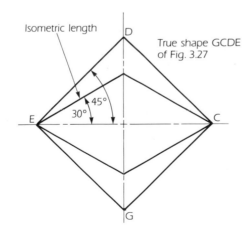
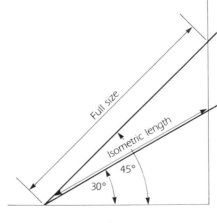

An isometric scale

Fig. 3.28

PERSPECTIVE PROJECTION

Perspective projection is used by architects and designers to illustrate
an object, such as a building, in a realistic manner. Artists also use
this form of drawing. It in fact makes parallel edges or lines appear
to converge towards a point in the distance. The larger the object the
more noticeable the converging effect becomes.

One-point perspective

This is the simplest form where the
parallel edges appear to meet at one
vanishing point, for example a long
straight stretch of railway track.

A rectangular block may be depicted
in one-point perspective by drawing
a front view and then selecting a
suitable vanishing point (VP),
projecting the depth towards this
point, as in Fig. 3.29.

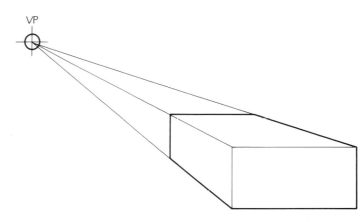

Fig. 3.29

Study the drawing of a room in Fig. 3.30 and you will notice that the
vanishing point has been positioned in the centre of the rear wall,
with all the lines being directed to this point. You will also note that
all the lines that do not go into the distance are drawn vertically or
horizontally.

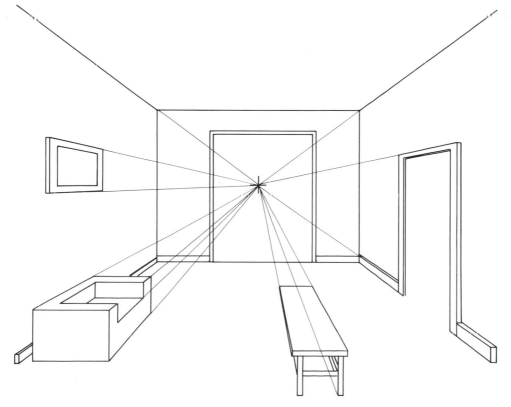

Fig. 3.30

Two-point perspective

In this form of projection there are two vanishing points. Now let us take a similar rectangular block to that in Fig. 3.29. You will observe in Fig. 3.31 that the perspective view adds realism to the drawing, with the line joining the two vanishing points corresponding to *eye level* (the horizon).

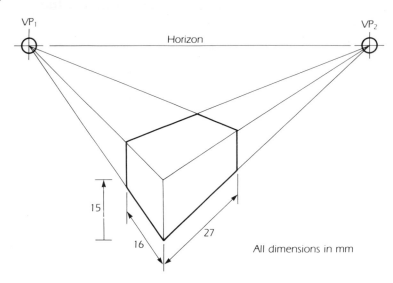

Fig. 3.31

Fig. 3.32 shows various projections of the same rectangular box.

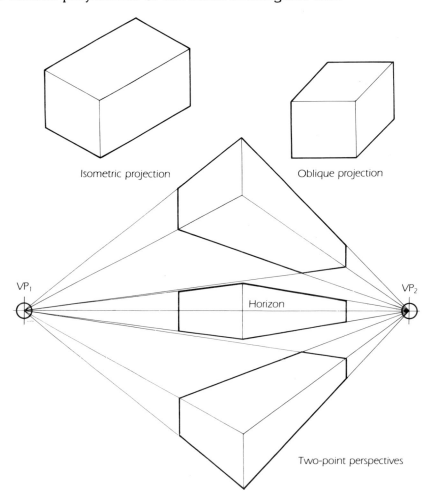

Fig. 3.32

EXERCISES

1. *You are a member of a firm of architects and you have been supplied with an axonometric sketch (Fig. 3.33) and a site plan (Fig. 3.34) of a family residence situated in a pleasant residential area of a city.*
    You have been requested to submit a design for a proposed extension which has to accommodate the following requirements:
    a) *a balcony that is facing east and situated on the first floor.*
    b) *a lounge that leads on to the balcony.*
    c) *a kitchenette containing a two-ring hob, two wall cupboards, inset sink and separate drainer, refrigerator, base units and a small breakfast bar suitable for two persons.*
    d) *a bedroom of double size incorporating a vanity basin and built-in wardrobe.*

    The building has to be built to the standard dwelling-place standards as set out by the local authority, and be of brick construction to correspond to the brickwork of the existing structure. A flat roof is permissible. Energy conservation has to be seriously considered in order to minimise the overall costs of heating and lighting. Garage parking has also to be incorporated in the design, with accommodation for four cars.
    The costs for this type of building are currently estimated to be £300/m² of the surface area, based upon the ground floor area measured externally. This figure includes the fees charged by the architect and all the materials that are required to complete the structure, including having the walls and ceilings emulsioned so that it is ready for occupation.
    The local planning authority has specified that there are the following constraints on the design:
    i) *no part of the building must exceed 4.5 m in height, excluding the roof.*
    ii) *no additional entrance/exit is permitted.*
    iii) *no part of the new extension may project beyond the building line of the existing property.*

Fig. 3.33

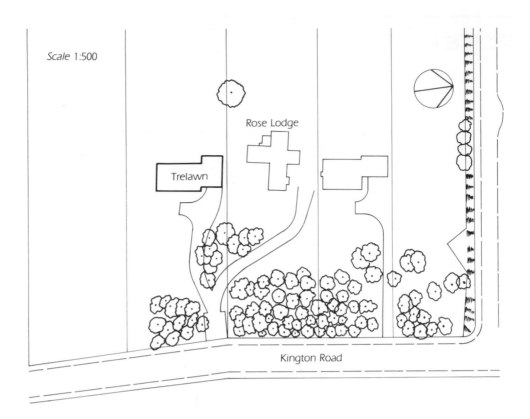

Scale 1:500

Rose Lodge

Trelawn

Kington Road

Fig. 3.34

2. *Kitchen planning has become an important part of modern-day life, in which efficiency, ease of maintenance and economy are major considerations. Analyse the movement within your own kitchen at home in order to make the environment more practical and generally more safe to work in.*

Make a scale drawing of your kitchen. Carefully watch a member of your family preparing a simple meal or drink, e.g. breakfast or a cup of coffee. On your kitchen plan, plot the directional movements with arrowed and numbered lines.

Analyse your drawings and comment upon the efficiency of the kitchen layout. From your analysis, redesign the kitchen using the existing fittings and furniture so that people using the kitchen will have a more efficient working environment and less walking to do.

Present your design as:

a) a one-point perspective drawing, and

b) a plan to scale of the redesigned kitchen.

Examples are shown in Fig. 3.35.

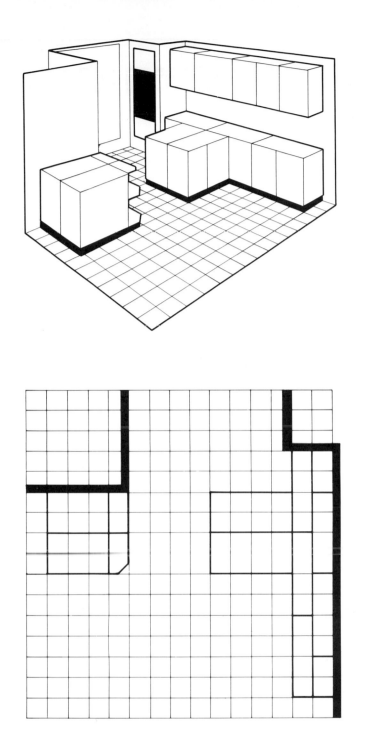

Fig. 3.35

Circuit Diagrams

A **circuit diagram** is a drawing that illustrates the direction and path or circuit of a medium that is moving under pressure.

There are two essential items that are needed in a circuit diagram:
a) symbols to represent the different controls within the circuit, and
b) a representation of the path along which the medium travels.

The BSI (see p. 72) has several publications that set out the specific symbols for use when drawing electrical circuits, hydraulic circuits and water systems that are used, for example, in the home. Stencils of these symbols may be used to keep them the same throughout the drawing of the particular circuit. Should there be no specific symbol to represent a unit in a particular circuit, then the constructor may invent a symbol for drawing purposes, but it is vitally important to produce a table of symbols somewhere on the drawing. The invented table of symbols is known as a **legend**.

EXAMPLE

Draw a circuit diagram for an electric light that is to be situated on a hall landing and operating on a 240 V circuit. The light is to be controlled by two two-way switches, one at either end of the landing. See Fig. 3.36, which uses BS symbols. The live line has to go to one side of the bulb and the neutral to the other side of the bulb. The live line has also to be connected to the **common terminal** of one switch. The two **free terminals** are connected to the two free terminals of the second switch.

Work through the diagram and you will be able to appreciate the path of the current with each switch in the on and off positions.

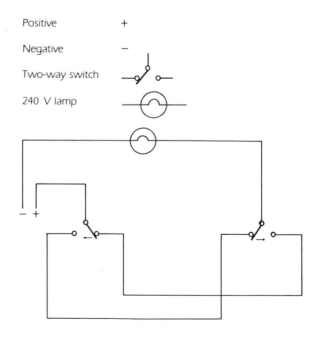

Positive   +

Negative   –

Two-way switch

240 V lamp

Fig. 3.36

Some BS electrical and electronic symbols are given below and on p. 98.

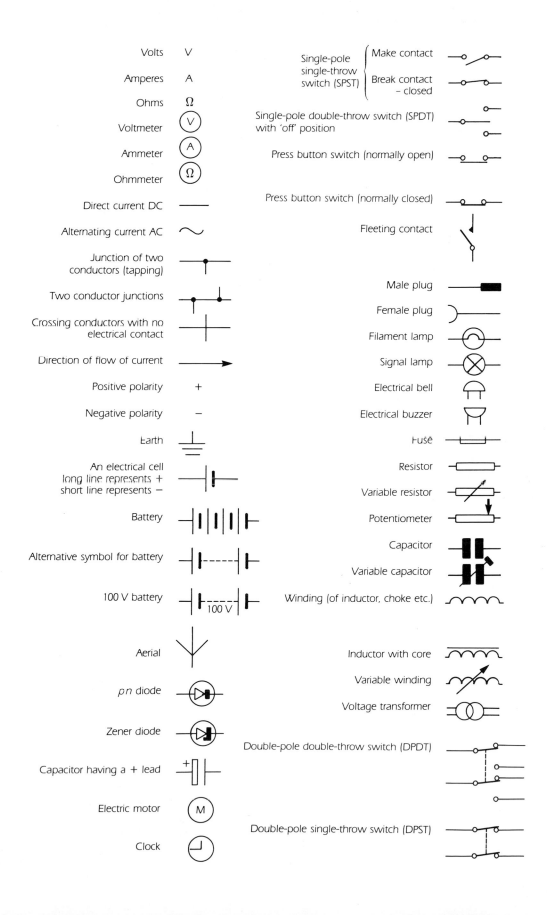

Volts	V	
Amperes	A	
Ohms	Ω	
Voltmeter		
Ammeter		
Ohmmeter		
Direct current DC		
Alternating current AC		
Junction of two conductors (tapping)		
Two conductor junctions		
Crossing conductors with no electrical contact		
Direction of flow of current		
Positive polarity	+	
Negative polarity	−	
Earth		
An electrical cell long line represents + short line represents −		
Battery		
Alternative symbol for battery		
100 V battery		
Aerial		
pn diode		
Zener diode		
Capacitor having a + lead		
Electric motor		
Clock		

Single-pole single-throw switch (SPST)
- Make contact
- Break contact – closed

Single-pole double-throw switch (SPDT) with 'off' position

Press button switch (normally open)

Press button switch (normally closed)

Fleeting contact

Male plug

Female plug

Filament lamp

Signal lamp

Electrical bell

Electrical buzzer

Fuse

Resistor

Variable resistor

Potentiometer

Capacitor

Variable capacitor

Winding (of inductor, choke etc.)

Inductor with core

Variable winding

Voltage transformer

Double-pole double-throw switch (DPDT)

Double-pole single-throw switch (DPST)

npn transistor

pnp transistor

Power transistor

Strain gauge

Operational amplifier (op amp)

Rotary switch (this example –
single-pole, six-way)

Fan

Chassis connection

Flashing light

Loudspeaker

EXAMPLES

Figs. 3.37–40 show examples of electronic circuits using BS symbols.

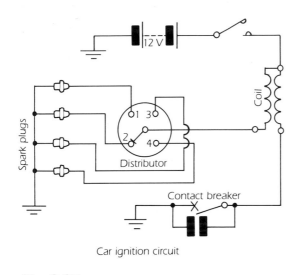

Car ignition circuit

Fig. 3.37

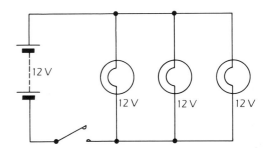

12 V bulbs light up when the switch is made.
Parallel circuit

Fig. 3.38

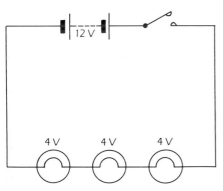

12 V battery will light three
4 V bulbs when the switch is made.
In series circuit

Fig. 3.39

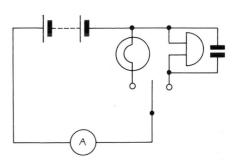

When the switch is to the right the bell will ring
and when it is to the left the bulb will light.
Battery connected with an ammeter in the circuit

Fig. 3.40

EXERCISES

1. *Use the correct electrical symbol for the indicated parts of the circuit in Fig. 3.41.*

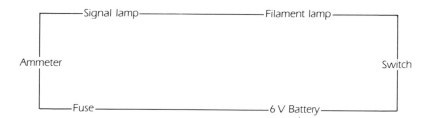

Fig. 3.41

2. *Replace the lettered parts of the circuits in Figs. 3.42–7 with the correct symbol.*

i) **Controlled circuit**
   a) *12 V battery*
   b) *SPST switch*
   c) *variable resistor*
   d) *signal lamp*
   e) *ammeter*
   f) *voltmeter*
   g) *filament bulb*

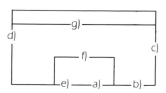

Fig. 3.42

ii) **Single lamp circuit**
   a) *4.5 V battery*
   b) *single-pole single-throw switch*
   c) *4.5 V lamp*

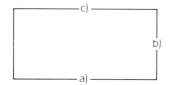

Fig. 3.43

iii) **Controlled electric motor circuit**
   a) *12 V DC electric motor*
   b) *0–15 V DC voltmeter*
   c) *0–1 A DC ammeter*
   d) *0–40 Ω variable resistance*

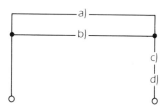

Fig. 3.44

iv) **Resistance circuit with ammeter**
   a) *3 V DC battery*
   b) *single-pole single-throw switch*
   c) *0–1 A DC ammeter*
   d) *5 Ω fixed value resistance*

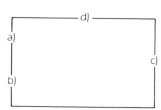

Fig. 3.45

v) **Rotary switched lamp circuit**
    a) *12 V AC supply*
    b) *three-pole rotary switch*
    c) *filament lamp 12 V 20 W*
    d) *filament lamp 12 V 10 W*
    e) *signal lamp 12 V 2.2 W*

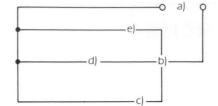

Fig. 3.46

vi) **Light-dependent resistor circuit**
    a) *12 000 Ω resistor*
    b) *strain gauge*
    c) *lamp*
    d) *n p n transistor*
    e) *power supply*

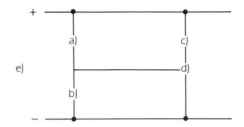

Fig. 3.47

3. *Make circuit drawings from the following data.*
   a) *Battery operated motor*
      12 V battery
      SPST switch
      12 V motor

   b) *A lamp with a variable resistance to control the brilliance*
      12 V battery
      SPST switch
      0–10 Ω variable resistance
      12 V 2.2 W lamp

   c) *Two lamps receiving power from a single battery*
      Single-pole double-throw switch
      6 V battery
      Two independently wired bulbs of 6 V 0.3 A

   d) *A system to operate an electric bell and a signal lamp*
      9 V supply
      SPST press button switch (normally open)
      9 V bell
      9 V 60 A signal lamp

4. *A house has a front doorbell and a buzzer at the rear door, with the power to both supplied by one 12 V transformer.*
   Design a circuit so that both sounding devices can be operated by a common supply and independently of each other.

5. *On many occasions you may be asked to convert a photograph or a sketch layout of electrical equipment into a circuit drawing.*
   Convert the diagrams in Figs. 3.48–50 into circuit diagrams.

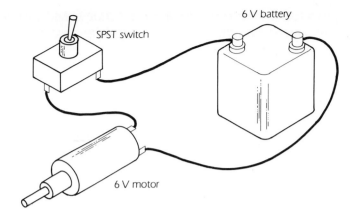

SPST switch

6 V battery

6 V motor

Fig. 3.48

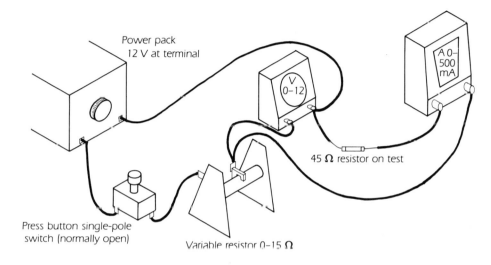

Power pack
12 V at terminal

V
0–12

A 0–
500
mA

45 Ω resistor on test

Press button single-pole
switch (normally open)

Variable resistor 0–15 Ω

Fig. 3.49

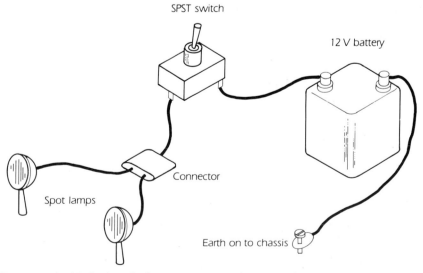

SPST switch

12 V battery

Connector

Spot lamps

Earth on to chassis

Headlamps attached to bodywork of car

Fig. 3.50

6. The sketch in Fig. 3.51 shows the electrical circuit that is used in an overhead projector. The fan is earthed to the supply through the case of the projector.

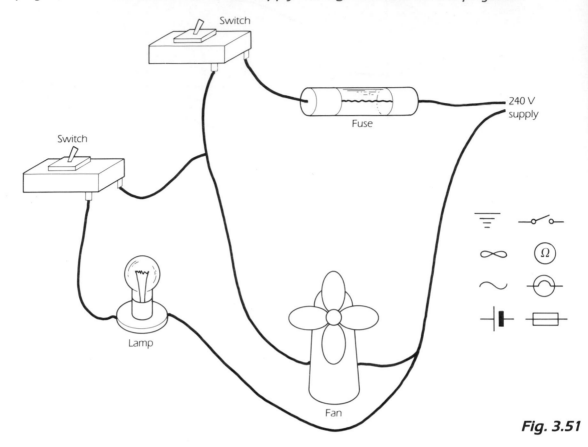

Fig. 3.51

Several electrical symbols are illustrated and from these you are requested to draw a wiring diagram of the given circuit.

7. Illustrated in Fig. 3.52 is the electrical circuit of a caravan which in operation is connected by means of a seven-pin plug to the battery of the towing vehicle. Draw a circuit diagram of the wiring of the caravan.

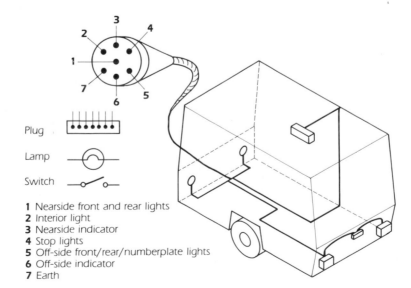

Plug

Lamp

Switch

1 Nearside front and rear lights
2 Interior light
3 Nearside indicator
4 Stop lights
5 Off-side front/rear/numberplate lights
6 Off-side indicator
7 Earth

Fig. 3.52

Pneumatics and Hydraulics

The use of **compressed air** and **hydraulic devices** to control the position of components is now commonplace. The doors of the majority of buses are opened and closed **pneumatically** and pneumatics operate automatic machinery in industry. The following gives the basis upon which most of these systems operate.

As we have seen in electronics, the use of symbols helps to eliminate vast amounts of detailed drawing and still allows one to understand the parts and components of the circuits.

DOUBLE-ACTING VALVES

The **double-acting valve** (shown in Fig. 3.53) is very similar to a bicycle pump, consisting of a metal **cylinder** in which a close-fitting **piston** moves from one end to the other. But unlike a bicycle pump a double-acting pneumatic cylinder has a fluid entry/exit hole at either end. This means that the piston can be pushed to either end of the cylinder by the injection of air behind it. The cylinder is therefore called double-acting because it can perform a function in either direction.

When the piston rod is fully out it is classified as **fully positive**.

When the piston rod is fully retracted into the cylinder it is classified as **fully negative.**

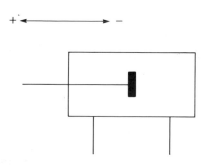

Fig. 3.53

THREE-PORT VALVES

The **three-port valve** (shown in Fig. 3.54) is the simplest type of
valve that controls the flow of compressed fluid and also allows the
exhausting fluid to escape when necessary. Because the valve has
two states which have different properties the valve is always
graphically illustrated showing the two functions. In Fig. 3.54, the
left-hand half of the diagram illustrates what happens when the
button is pressed, and the right-hand half what happens when the
button is not pressed.

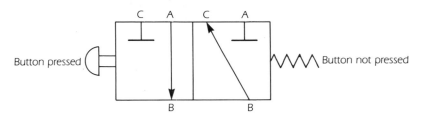

Fig. 3.54

The three ports, A, B and C, are the entry and exit holes in the side
of the valve. The type of valve illustrated has an operating button on
the side and an internal spring that pushes the button up when the
pressure is released.

In the right-hand half of Fig. 3.54, **inlet port** A is blocked inside the
valve and therefore it is not possible for the compressed fluid to pass
through the valve to port B. But it is possible for fluid to escape from
port B through the valve to port C and into the atmosphere or
reservoir. This **flow path** is illustrated on a valve by a solid line, in
this case the line joining B and C.

When the button is pressed down the compressed fluid at port A is
allowed to pass through the valve to port B and the exhaust port
(outlet) at C is now blocked.

A circle with a dot in the centre (see Fig. 3.55) is the simplified
general symbol that represents an energy conversion unit, a
compressor, a **pump** or a **motor**.

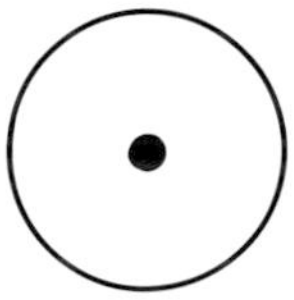

Fig. 3.55

EXAMPLE

A double-acting cylinder is connected through
one inlet to two three-port valves, A and B, in
series. Both the valve buttons must be pressed
in order to make the piston
fully positive. The top half
of Fig. 3.56 illustrates that
with both the buttons
pressed the fluid passes
through the valves.

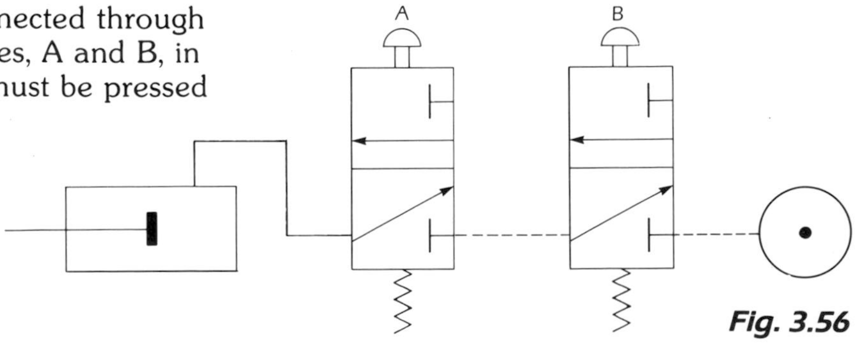

Fig. 3.56

Two three-port valves, A and B, are required to operate a double-acting cylinder, shown in Fig. 3.57. The lower half of the diagram shows both valves being used without the buttons pressed, and because of this both sides of the piston are exhausted. If the button on valve A is now depressed the valve changes over, and the top half of the diagram of the valve illustrates what happens. The compressed air or fluid is passed through the valve and makes the piston positive with the fluid in front of the piston being exhausted through valve B. If valve A is then released and the valve B button pressed the piston will go negative.

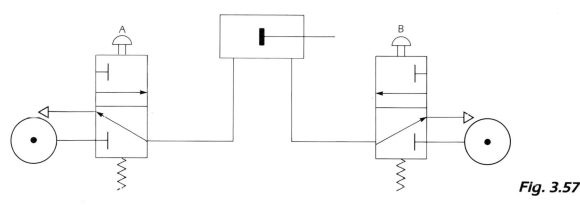

Fig. 3.57

Should both buttons be pressed at the same time the piston will not move because an equal pressure is being applied to both sides of the piston.

FIVE-PORT VALVES

The **five-port valve** (shown in Fig. 3.58) can be used to hold a piston firmly in the positive or negative position even if the controlling signal is removed. This type of valve has two ports, B and D, that are connected directly to the cylinder with port A receiving the fluid supply from the pressure source. The fluid entering at port A is switched either to port B or to port D. When the compressed fluid is switched to port B, port D is connected to port E and then exhausted. The piston is then negative.

To make the piston go positive the valve must change over, and the left-hand side of the diagram of the valve illustrates what happens. Study the diagram and you will see that when the valve is in the state shown in the right-hand half, the piston goes negative, and when it is in the state shown in the left-hand half, the piston goes positive.

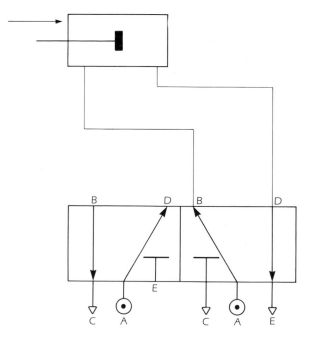

Fig. 3.58

SINGLE-ACTING CYLINDER

The **single-acting cylinder** (shown in Fig. 3.59) is similar to the double-acting cylinder in construction except that there is only one input/output port and the piston is driven negative by a spring.

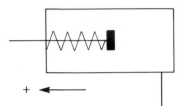

Fig. 3.59

When fluid is supplied to the port the piston is pushed into a positive position with the amount of compression being proportional to the force applied. Therefore a single-acting cylinder driven through a pressure regulator (see the next section) will automatically become a continuous control device, whereas a double-acting cylinder acts more like a switch as the piston is driven from one end of the cylinder to the other.

PRESSURE REGULATOR

A **pressure regulator** (shown in Fig. 3.60) is a device that will reduce the pressure applied to it. It can be adjusted to deliver a constant preset output pressure providing that the input pressure never drops below the output pressure.

The compressed fluid input is switched through to an output connection until the output pressure rises to a preset level controlled by an adjustable spring inside the regulator. When that pressure is reached the input is shut off by the compressed spring. If the output pressure falls the regulator allows more of the input fluid through it until the output pressure rises to the set value controlled by the spring. Should the output pressure rise too high the regulator will allow some fluid to escape backwards from the output to the exhaust or reservoir.

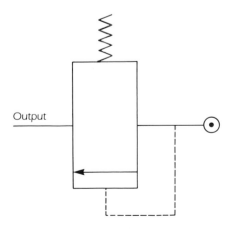

Fig. 3.60

EXERCISES

1. *Fig. 3.61 shows a controlled system to deliver a predetermined quantity of potatoes into a sack. Name the types of valves that are used in the system.*

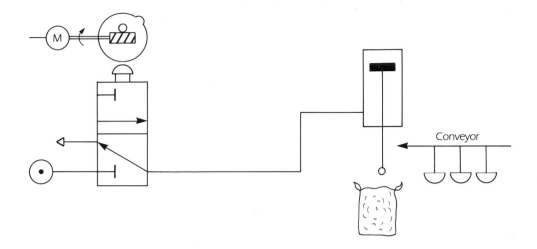

Fig. 3.61

2. *Fig. 3.62 is a simple outline of a drilling machine and it has been suggested that it can be automatically controlled.*

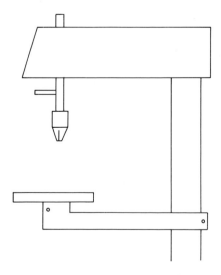

Fig. 3.62

You are requested to link up the valves given in Fig. 3.63 in a manner that will allow the machine to drill a large number of holes to an automatically controlled depth.

The valves available are:

a) double-acting valve;
b) two off three-port valves; and
c) one off double-acting cylinder.

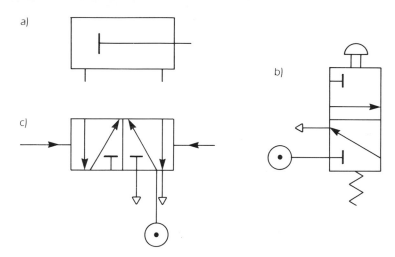

Fig. 3.63

3. Consider other pieces of machinery within the workshop that could be automatically controlled.

    Have you thought of controlling the windows in a greenhouse to accommodate the change in temperature?

    What about automatically opening doors?

    Attempt to draw control circuits for the above problems.

Symbols at Home

A language in graphics for *effective* communication has useful applications in the home, for example when making decisions about washing, decorating, gardening or buying food.

Washing Symbols

In washing clothes and fabrics it is essential that we should know the correct temperature for the water, otherwise the fabric may stretch or shrink. Likewise for ironing or non-ironing; maybe the garment has to be allowed to drip-dry for best results, and ironing could be harmful. The symbols in Figs. 4.1 and 4.2 provide useful information on textile care in a standard short form. They show a new set of symbols in use from August 1987.

Hand wash only	May be tumble dried	Cool iron
Do not wash at all	Do not tumble dry	Warm iron
Do not dry clean	Do not use household bleach	Hot iron
Dry clean only	Household bleach may be used (Follow manufacturer's instructions)	Do not iron

Fig. 4.1

Symbol	Textile/ machine code	Handwashing instructions	Examples of application
95	*Maximum* wash in cotton cycle	Hand hot (50°C) or boil Spin or wring	White cotton and linen articles without special finishes
60	*Maximum* wash in cotton cycle	Hand hot (50°C) Spin or wring	Cotton, linen or viscose articles without special finishes where colours are fast at 60°C
50	*Medium* wash in synthetics cycle	Hand hot Cold rinse, short spin or damp dry	Polyester/cotton mixtures, nylon, polyester; cotton and viscose articles with special finishes, cotton/acrylic mixtures

Symbol	Textile/ machine code	Handwashing instructions	Examples of application
⌷40⌷	*Maximum* wash in cotton cycle	Warm Spin or wring	Cotton, linen or viscose where colours are fast at 40°C but not at 60°C
⌷40⌷	*Medium* wash in synthetics cycle	Warm Cold rinse, short spin, do not hand wring	Acrylics, acetate and triacetate; including mixtures with wool; polyester/wool blends
⌷40⌷	*Minimum* wash in wool cycle	Warm Do not rub, short spin, do not hand wring	Wool, wool mixed with other fibres; silk

Articles labelled ⌷8/30⌷ or ⌷30⌷ should be washed in the appropriate (40°C) MEDIUM or MINIMUM cycle or hand washed.

Fig. 4.2

EXERCISES

1. *List the meanings of all the graphic instructions in Fig. 4.3.*
   Look at other garments and fabrics and see if you can find any different
   combinations of the standard symbols.

Used for: 100% cotton

100% cotton with special finishes

65% polyester, 35% viscose

Coloured nylon

60% lambswool, 20% angora, 20% nylon/polyamide

55% polyester, 45% wool

Fig. 4.3

Wallpapering Symbols

The Wallcovering Manufacturers' Association has now recommended the progressive introduction of the international performance symbols in the United Kingdom, and over the next few years we will see the symbols in Figs. 4.4 and 4.5 coming more into use in wallpaper pattern books and on the product labels.

Try to interpret the graphic instructions in Fig. 4.4, and then check your answers against the full list of symbols in Fig. 4.5.

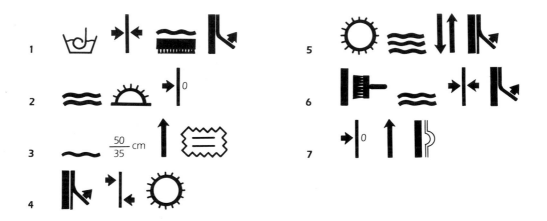

Fig. 4.4

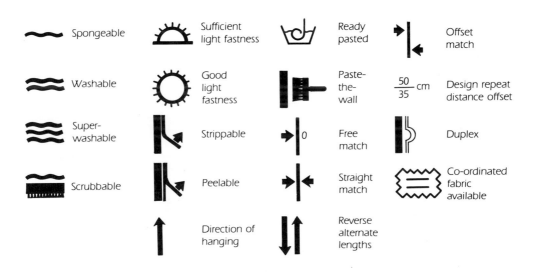

Fig. 4.5

Packing Case Symbols

With the transit of goods throughout the world via land, sea and air, there is a need for instructions on packing cases that can be interpreted by anybody, no matter which language they speak. The symbols in Fig. 4.6 have been developed to answer this need.

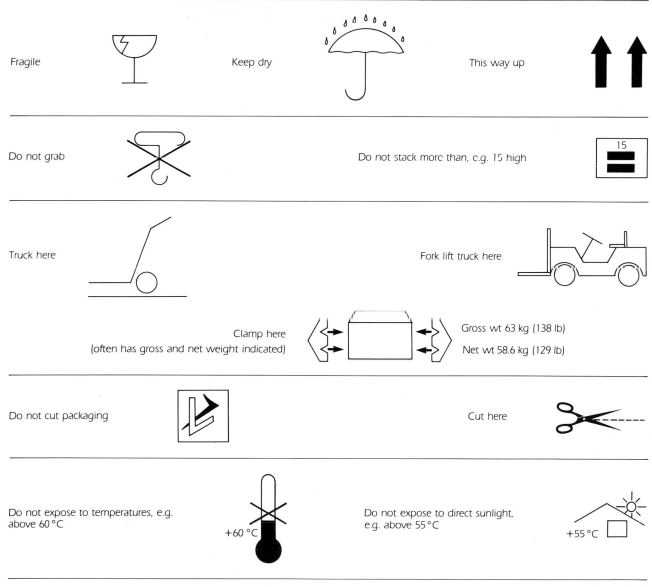

Fragile

Keep dry

This way up

Do not grab

Do not stack more than, e.g. 15 high

Truck here

Fork lift truck here

Clamp here
(often has gross and net weight indicated)

Gross wt 63 kg (138 lb)

Net wt 58.6 kg (129 lb)

Do not cut packaging

Cut here

Do not expose to temperatures, e.g. above 60 °C
+60 °C

Do not expose to direct sunlight, e.g. above 55 °C
+55 °C

Fig. 4.6

These symbols can be found on the majority of packaging, not necessarily exactly as illustrated here but in the same general format. When the information has a **Do not**, for example, the symbol is usually covered by a bold cross, as indicated by the **Do not grab** symbol.

Fig. 4.7 shows packaging symbols being consulted by a handler. The symbols are very prominent on the carton so that storage and handling requirements can quickly be assessed in the warehouse.

Fig. 4.7

EXERCISES

1. *Illustrate graphically the symbols that you would use on the packaging of the following products:*

washing machine	*grandfather clock*
stereo unit	*cast iron bath*
slow cooker	*shower door*
packing case of Edinburgh crystal	*7-metre fibreglass sloop*
built-in oven unit	*2-tonne roll of newsprint*
engineers' lathe	*square carton of rag dolls 1 m by 1 m*
microprocessor	*bushel of apples*
television	

The Garden Centre

The garden centre might seem to be a rather odd place to look for information graphics, but today more and more symbols are being used there, as elsewhere, to help the general public to determine specific reference material quickly. Fig. 4.8 lists only a few of these symbols.

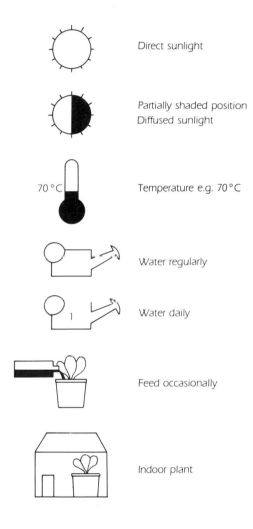

Direct sunlight

Partially shaded position
Diffused sunlight

Temperature e.g. 70 °C

Water regularly

Water daily

Feed occasionally

Indoor plant

Fig. 4.8

EXERCISES

1.   *Develop the list in Fig. 4.8 by adding further symbols that might assist the gardener.*

Food Symbols

Next time that you visit the chemist's or maybe a health food store look carefully at the dietary information that is given on the packaging of vitamins, minerals and health foods by means of the symbols in Fig. 4.9.

Artificial additive-free		Vegetarian	
Low sodium		Milk-free	
Refined sugar-free		Egg-free	
Cholesterol-free		Grain-free	
Low saturated fat		Gluten-free (no wheat, rye, barley or oats)	

Fig. 4.9

EXERCISES

1. *Make a list of the products that use the symbols in Fig. 4.9 to help the public identify specific information relating to the food product.*

Symbols for Illustrations

Many events are happening about us during our daily lives, and we often need to be able to represent these movements graphically. A recognised system has been evolved and is shown in Fig. 4.10. It is used on drawings to avoid having to describe the movement in clumsy sentences. As an example, vision line is used when describing the operation of looking through a magnifying glass to identify a small article. One-way movement can be seen on Fig. 6.16 p. 141, illustrating the direction of movement of a compass.

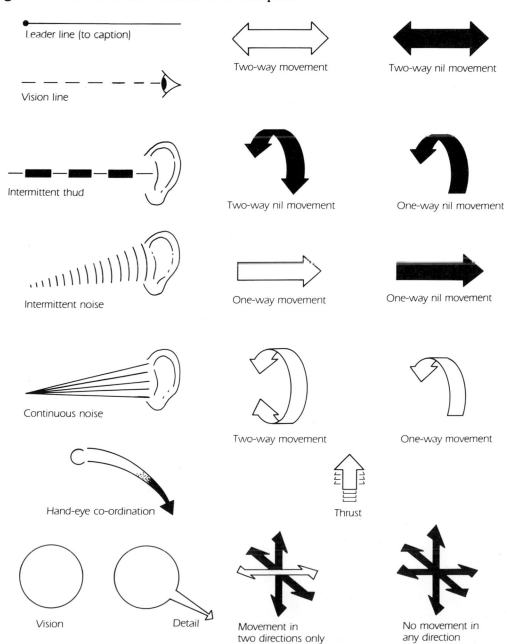

Fig. 4.10

Signs

Graphics come very much to the forefront when a message needs to be quickly and clearly conveyed. Particular examples considered here are signs concerned in various ways with safety, such as signs for fire fighting, dangerous substances and vehicle markings.

The Law and Signs

On January 1, 1981, new legislation came into effect governing the design of some safety signs. The need for this legislation was a result of a directive from the EEC in July 1977. It is now obligatory to display a sign that is controlled by these regulations, and it must conform by law to BS 5378 Part 1. The directive does not determine where a sign should be displayed, but the obligations to do this are governed by the Health and Safety at Work Act, 1974.

The signs on the following charts conform to BS 5378. Some of them are symbol signs (**pictograms**) without text. There are also supplementary signs, which are signs with text only and may be used in conjunction with pictograms providing that the text is apart from the symbol and does not interfere with the symbol.

Fig. 5.1 shows the principles of colour and design for the different types of safety sign adopted by BS 5378.

Fig. 5.1

The following pages show examples of these different types.

PROHIBITION SIGNS

All prohibition signs are red and white. These signs contain a red circle with a diagonal line through it, and the lettering is white upon a red background mounted on white. See Fig. 5.2.

 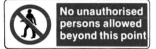 

 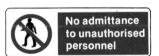 

 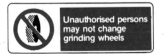 

Fig. 5.2

WARNING SIGNS

All warning signs are based upon the colours black and yellow, with the main instruction always being printed in black on a yellow background. See Fig. 5.3.

 Highly flammable L.P.G.

 Nitric acid

 Danger high voltage

 Highly flammable

 Sulphuric acid

 Danger live wires

 Highly flammable liquid

 Caustic soda

 Danger bare live wires

 Danger highly flammable store

 Hydrochloric acid

 Danger overhead cables

 Cyanide

 Danger men working on this circuit

 Danger 415 volts

 Ammonia

 Danger live busbars

 Danger 440 volts

 Toxic

 Danger buried cable

 Danger 11,000 volts

Corrosive

 Mind your head

 Danger switch off when not in use

Fig. 5.3

MANDATORY SIGNS

All mandatory signs are based upon a blue background with white instructions. See Fig. 5.4.

 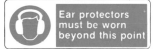 

Fig. 5.4

SAFE CONDITION SIGNS

All safe condition signs have a green background with the instruction
always in white. See Fig. 5.5.

FIRE EXIT

EMERGENCY EXIT ONLY

Slide to open

Assembly point

FIRE EXIT KEEP CLEAR

EXIT

Push to open

Slide to open →

Pull to open

Fire escape

In case of fire break glass bolt to open

Slide to open ←

In case of fire break glass for key

EMERGENCY EXIT

Push bar to open

Fire escape light switch

First aid

Eye wash

Eye wash

Breathing apparatus

Drinking water

Smoking permitted

First aid

Drinking water

Emergency Stop

First aid station

FIRE EXIT ONLY

Eye wash

FIRST AID
THE PERSON ON DUTY IS

IF ABSENT

OUR TRAINED FIRST AIDER IS-

First aid kit carried

Emergency shower

Stretcher

Fig. 5.5

FIRE FIGHTING SIGNS

All fire fighting signs have a red background with white lettering, with the exception of the signs that are placed upon fire extinguishers. These indicate the contents and when the appliance should be used in relation to the type of fire and where the fire is situated. See Fig. 5.6.

Fire alarm

Fire extinguisher

Fire-hose reel

Fire hydrant

Fire phone

Fire alarm

Fire extinguisher

Fire hose

Foam inlet

Fire alarm call point

Fire alarm inside

Fire point

Fire hose reel

Dry riser

In case of fire switch off here

Fire switch

Fire hydrant

Fire hose must be kept clear

Wet riser

Fire buckets

In case of fire sound alarm

Fire hydrant keep clear

Fire extinguisher must be kept clear

Sprinkler control valve

Break glass in case of fire

TYPES OF MODERN FIRE EXTINGUISHERS

B S I DD48 1976

WATER
USE FOR WOOD PAPER FABRICS ETC
DO NOT USE ON ELECTRICAL OR FLAMMABLE LIQUID FIRES

FOAM
USE FOR FLAMMABLE LIQUIDS OILS FATS SPIRITS ETC
DO NOT USE ON ELECTRICAL FIRES

POWDER
USE FOR ALL RISKS FLAMMABLE LIQUIDS & GASES

CO_2
USE FOR ELECTRICAL & FLAMMABLE LIQUID FIRES

BCF
USE FOR ELECTRICAL & FLAMMABLE LIQUID FIRES

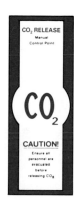
CO_2 RELEASE
Manual
Control Point
CO_2
CAUTION!
Ensure all personnel are evacuated before releasing CO_2

HALON RELEASE
Manual
Control Point
HALON
CAUTION!
Ensure all personnel are evacuated before releasing HALON

Fig. 5.6

DANGEROUS SUBSTANCES

The packaging and labelling of dangerous substances is extremely
important today, as various goods are transported to and from all
the corners of the earth by land, sea and air. It is therefore important
that the handlers of these many types of products have some
knowledge of the materials that they are transporting in case of
possible leakage, breakage, fire or explosion. Signs for this purpose
are shown in Fig. 5.7.

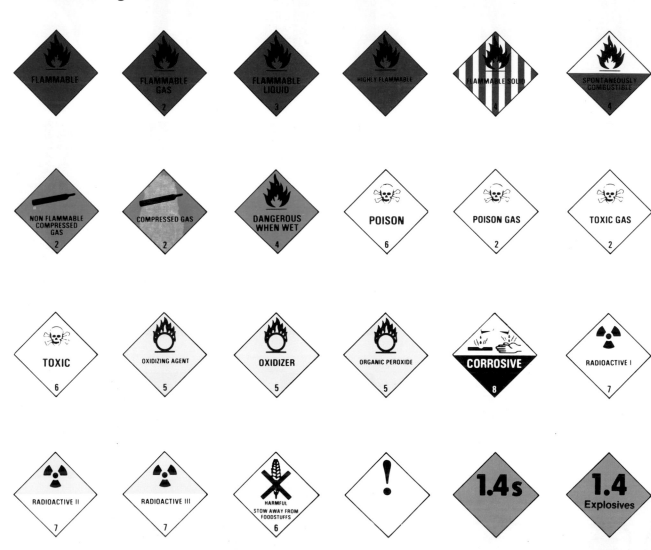

Fig. 5.7

The signs illustrated in Fig. 5.8 show precautions that must be taken when handling particular types of substances. The visual display warns people dealing with the substance of the type of precaution to be taken, even if they cannot understand the English notation which is on the majority of the signs. These signs can often be seen on the rear of many lorries today, especially tankers. The details of the contents and an emergency telephone number are given along with the visual display which is positioned in the large major block of the sign on the left-hand side. The example illustrated here is 'HARMFUL'.

The visual display signs always have an orange background with the sign and lettering in black.

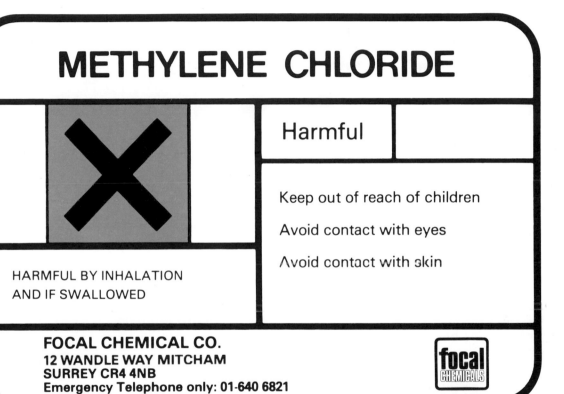

Fig. 5.8

Vehicle Markings

HEAVY GOODS VEHICLE REAR MARKINGS

Motor-vehicles over 7500 kilograms maximum gross weight and
trailers over 3500 kilograms maximum gross weight show the signs
in Fig. 5.9.

Left   Right

Fig. 5.9

Commercial vehicles or combinations longer than 13 metres (optional
on combinations between 11 and 13 metres) show the signs in
Fig. 5.10.

Left   Right   or

Fig. 5.10

PROJECTION MARKERS

These are required when the
load or the equipment on a
vehicle overhangs the front or
rear of the vehicle by more than
1.83 m. They would be used,
for example, for a crane jib. The
markers are shown in Fig. 5.11.

Fig. 5.11

General Signs

The general signs illustrated on this page are signs that are recommended for use only in the UK and are not required to be shown by law. The signs suggest a common style to be used generally so that the public appreciates what information is being suggested or recommended. General signs are always black instructions upon a white background, with the exception of the signs that indicate a speed limit that is under the recognised 30 mph public highway limit. These signs have a red circle around the indicated speed. See Fig. 5.12.

Notice this entrance must be kept clear

Private **car park**	**Notice** **no parking in** **this area**	**Goods** **inwards**	**Notice** Vehicles and contents are left here entirely at owner's risk

Car park	**No parking**	**Goods** **outwards**	**All drivers** **and visitors** **must report** **to gatehouse**

Visitors **car park**	**No parking** **beyond this** **point**	**All drivers** **and visitors** **must report** **to reception**	**Motorway** **Maintenance**

Visitors **only**	**No parking in** **front of these** **gates**	**Safety Notice** This area must be kept clear for emergency vehicles	It is the responsibility of the driver to ensure that passengers do not travel on this vehicle

Fig. 5.12

Tapes

HAZARD AND SAFETY TAPES

These tapes are manufactured in a tough, flexible, waterproof material, in either self-adhesive or non-adhesive forms. They are suitable for use both indoors or outside. Under the direction of the 1981 legislation these tapes should be used as follows.

1   Warning – black and yellow
    a) to identify mobile equipment which may cause hazards, i.e. fork-lift trucks
    b) to identify uneven floor surfaces or a change in the levels
    c) to identify obstructions, low headroom, machine guards etc.

2   Prohibition – red and white
    a) to identify the location of all fire-fighting equipment
    b) to identify the location or position of emergency stop buttons or handles etc.
    c) to highlight the position of non-smoking notices in dangerous areas

3   Emergency – green and white
    a) to identify the location of safety equipment, first aid posts, eye wash units etc.
    b) to identify fire and emergency exits

Fig. 5.13

PACKAGING TAPES

1   Urgent – white on red
2   Fragile – red on white
3   Electrical wiring – black on white
4   Sample – blue on white
5   Invoice enclosed – red on white
6   Reject – black on yellow
7   Advice note enclosed – red on white
8   No flammable liquid or gas – red on white

Colours of wiring indicated:
green/yellow, earth
brown, live
blue, neutral

Fig. 5.14

Orange Badge Scheme

People who are disabled can apply to their local council for a special windscreen badge, shown in Fig. 5.15. If this badge is clearly displayed on their vehicles, it will grant them special parking concessions.

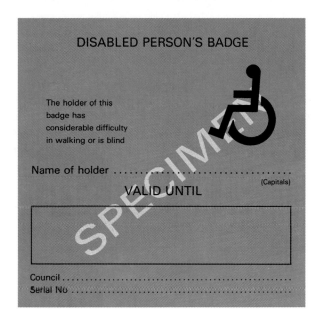

DISABLED PERSON'S BADGE

The holder of this
badge has
considerable difficulty
in walking or is blind

Name of holder . . . .

(Capitals)

VALID UNTIL

SPECIMEN

Council . . . .
Serial No . . . .

Fig. 5.15

EXERCISES

1. *Make enquiries and discover what concessions are granted by your local council to disabled people.*

2. *Concessions are now available to disabled drivers when buying a new car from some leading manufacturers. Make enquiries locally to find out what deals are on offer, and what types of conversion are avilable. You might then like to forward this information on to somebody you know who could make use of your research.*

Design a Sign

EXERCISES

1. *This book looks at many of the signs that are produced for our advantage: warning the general public and employees in all walks of life of work that is being undertaken, or of possible dangers; giving advice on looking after themselves or what to do in an emergency; giving general advice, directions, or information about facilities.*

   Design a sign for use specifically in the Craft, Design and Technology department of your school or college. Look carefully at the working environment and make a list of the areas that you think would benefit from a sign placed there. Consider all the possible hazards that are in the workshops. How about the access to these buildings?

   When you have made your list, consider the content of the sign. What type of sign will it be? Will the sign be a warning, prohibition, mandatory, safe condition, general, or fire fighting sign, or should a product be labelled?

2. *Devise a road sign for use on a motorway to convey the message that 1 mile further along the road are facilities for refuelling and refreshments. The sign should be different from existing signs and both colour and format should be carefully considered.*

   Make initial sketches of your design, and consider your sign's position and its siting by the motorway. Make sketches of the method of assembly of the sign, and plan the finished sign's overall dimensions. Then make a scale drawing of your final design, and illustrate it in either isometric or oblique projection. Finally, make a scale model of your sign using available materials.
   N.B. *Any joints on your model should be properly constructed, e.g. halving joints.*

3. *British Rail have commissioned you to design signs to be placed above the passenger entry and exit doors on their railway carriages.*

   The information that they wish you to convey in the form of symbols is:

   a) Do not open the door when the train is moving.

   b) Danger, do not lean out of the window.

   The maximum size of each sign is 75 mm × 75 mm, and they must be limited to two colours.

Developments

Taking graphic communication one step towards the stages of realisation, we now investigate ways in which three-dimensional representations or models may be planned and constructed. In the design process, model making is a logical development from drawing, and enables the design to be more thoroughly visualised and appraised.

Surface Developments

One important aspect of technical graphics is that of **surface developments**. The surface development of an object is a precise flat shape that may be folded, bent or rolled in order to produce a three dimensional solid model of the object.

Consider an envelope. The development, shown in Fig. 6.1, consists of a rectangular panel which becomes the front, two triangular ends, one triangular flap and one truncated flap. The ends fold around as the sides and the flaps form the enclosure, with the top flap being gummed during manufacture and shaped so that it overlaps the end two panels.

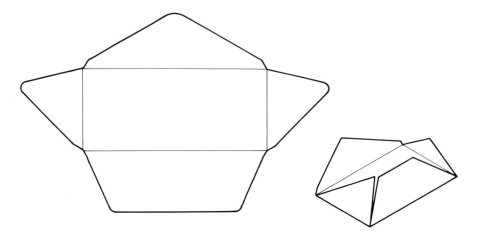

Fig. 6.1

Another example of surface development, taken from the clothing industry is the sleeve of a jacket. The pattern is placed on the fabric and the shape is cut around. The fabric is then rolled and stitched along the prescribed lines, as shown in Fig. 6.2.

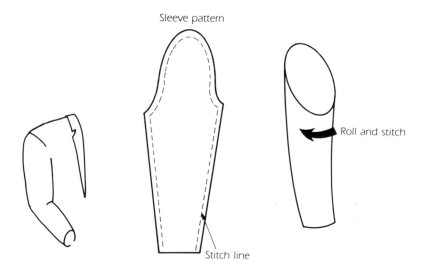

Sleeve pattern

Roll and stitch

Stitch line

Fig. 6.2

The simplest form of development is a square box or a cuboid,
which is a box that has square ends and rectangular sides like the
one shown in Fig. 6.3.

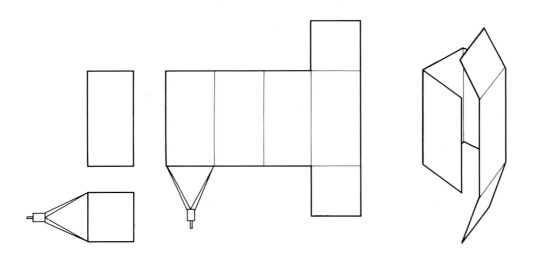

Fig. 6.3

Take a typical breakfast cereal packet and open it out flat. With
boxes and cartons being made in this way the printing can be
carried out on the flat surface, which is far easier than trying to
print on a completed carton.

Another form of development is that of a square-based pyramid, the
development being formed by a number of radial lines, each of them
representing one corner of the shape. You can see in Fig. 6.4 that the
square-based pyramid is made up of a group of four triangles on a
square base, meeting together at the apex.

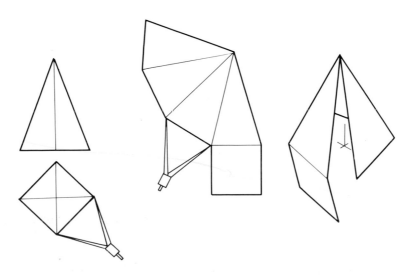

Fig. 6.4

Fig. 6.5 shows the development by triangulation of a transition piece that has a square base and a circular top. You can see that the development has straight lines at the outside edges and a curved one at the inside edges.

A transition piece is used to join circular pipes or ducting to square pipes or ducting.

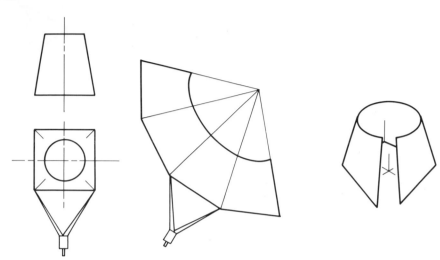

Fig. 6.5

EXERCISES

1. *Construct, using compasses or dividers, the following prisms. You are given the front elevation and plan, and are required to reproduce the prisms to your own dimensions.*
   a) Square prism (Fig. 6.6)

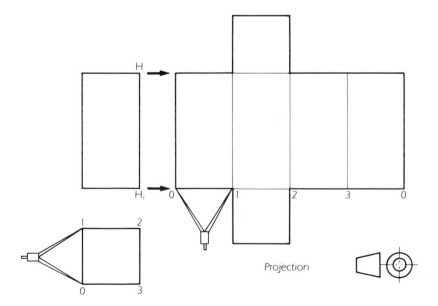

Projection

Fig. 6.6

b) Irregular prism (Fig. 6.7)

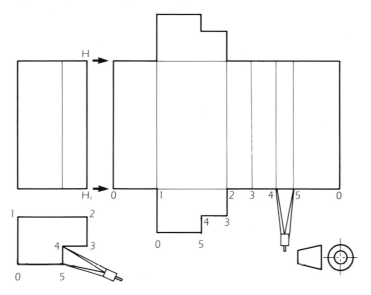

Fig. 6.7

c) Cylinder (Fig. 6.8)

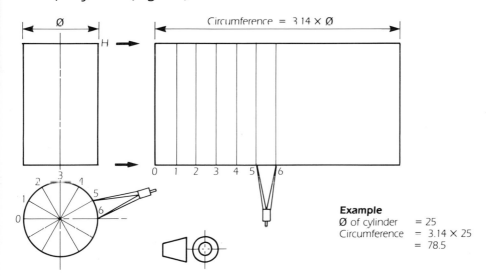

Example

Ø of cylinder	= 25
Circumference	= 3.14 × 25
	= 78.5

Fig. 6.8

d) Prism with sloping surface (Fig. 6.9)

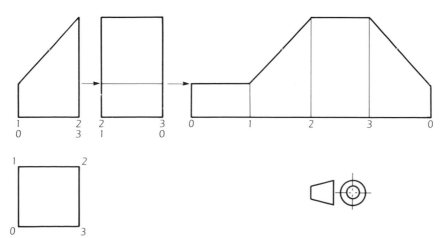

Fig. 6.9

TRUE SHAPES OF INCLINED PLANES

To obtain the true shape of the sloping surface of the prism in
Fig. 6.9, the surface has to be viewed at 90°, as illustrated in
Fig. 6.10.

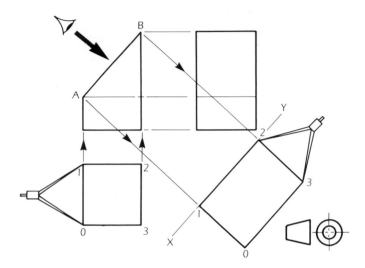

Fig. 6.10

The direction of view in Fig. 6.10 is shown by an arrow perpendicular
to the surface A–B. A line X–Y is drawn parallel to A–B in a
convenient position and, using dividers, 0–1 is taken off the plan view
and set off perpendicular to the new line X–Y. The projection is then
completed, giving the true shape of the inclined surface.

Fig. 6.11 illustrates how the original prism with a sloping surface would
be drawn to enable it to be folded into a box. Glue tabs have been
omitted.

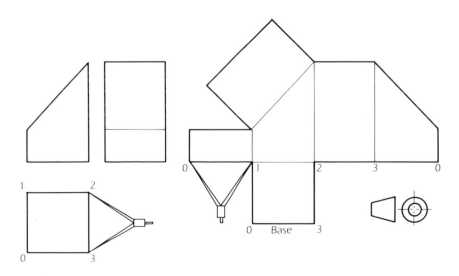

Fig. 6.11

Fig. 6.12 illustrates the development of a five-sided prism by projecting from the front elevation and stepping off the distances from the plan view.

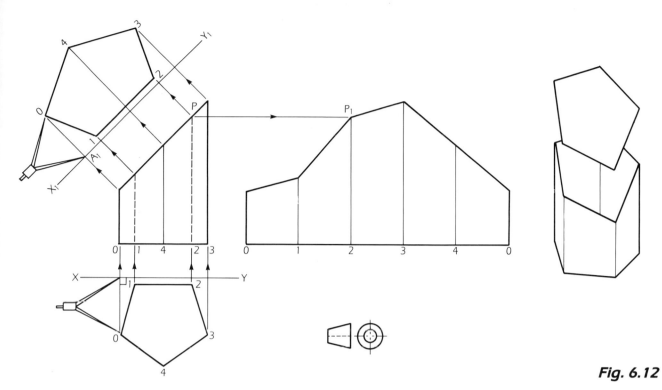

Fig. 6.12

Fig. 6.13 shows the method of obtaining the true shape of a truncated cylinder and the development of the circumference. The latter is obtained by stepping the distance $0-P_0$, $1-P_1$ etc. along the line $0-0$ on the development.

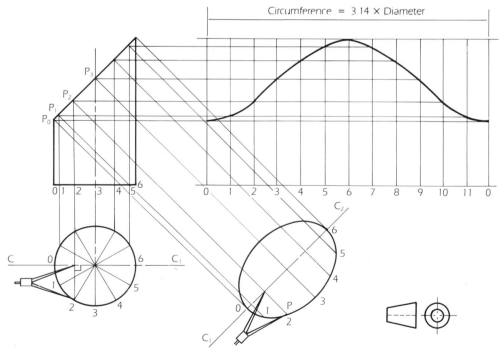

Fig. 6.13

Cardboard Engineering

Having spent many hours preparing designs and working drawings for project work, students often discover that their completed item is not quite as they originally intended, which causes general disappointment in their final product. A great deal of experience is required before a design can be realised from drawings with an assurance of success.

Optical illusion is often a problem that has to be overcome in ensuring that the final product looks just as it was originally conceived. A student's work may look ideal on the drawing board with well laid-out and presented working drawings, with perspective sketches colour washed to enhance the final appearance, but when constructed the design can look sometimes rather different.

To avoid this problem and the time wasted in the workshops, combined with the increase in overall cost of the finished item, a means must be adopted which allows for the checking of the shapes and forms in a design before a vast amount of expenditure is incurred. This is achieved through models which may be constructed in card, balsa wood, plastics or clay. They can be relatively quickly prepared and assist the appraisal of the product prior to the final manufacture.

This book looked earlier at surface developments and auxiliary views. This section concerns itself with constructions using sheet materials built from surface developments.

MODELLING TECHNIQUES

The quickest method of checking a drawing is by the use of a tracing. Take a sheet of good quality tracing paper and tape it down over the original drawing. Then using a sharp pencil and the appropriate drawing instrument trace the profile and the relevant details. This tracing can then be transferred on to any other type of card or paper as required. See Fig. 6.14.

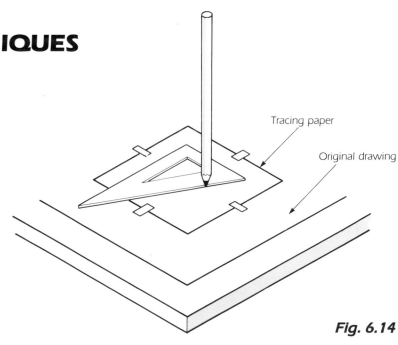

Tracing paper

Original drawing

Fig. 6.14

When the development for a model is composed entirely of straight lines it is possible to pierce through the original drawing on to a sheet of card by using a sharp pointed instrument like a divider point or a scriber, as shown in Fig. 6.15.

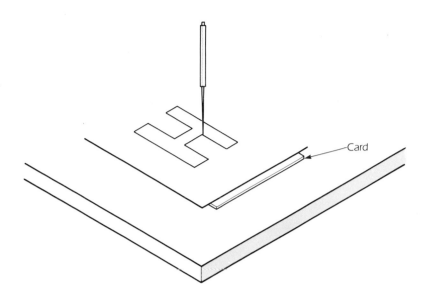

Card

Fig. 6.15

Should the model involve large diameters or curves the process used is to place carbon paper beneath the original drawing, or better still, beneath a copy of the original drawing on a lighter grade of paper, and then go over the required lines to transfer an impression on to the card via the carbon paper. See Fig. 6.16.

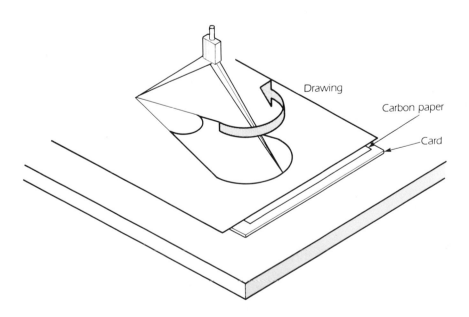

Drawing

Carbon paper

Card

Fig. 6.16

MODELLING ASSEMBLIES

When the shapes of the model are developments of cones or cylinders, assembly is simply a matter of carefully rolling the cutout and taping along the seam, or making allowances for a glue-tab along one edge, usually 3–6 mm in width, as in Fig. 6.17.

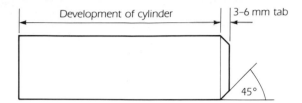

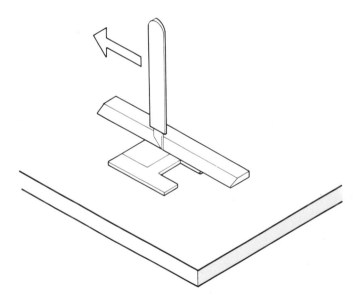

Fig. 6.17

When cutting out the pieces, skill is needed to use a craft knife and a steel straight edge. Work on a cutting board all the time. See Fig. 6.18.

Fig. 6.18

Should the card then need to be folded, make a score on the appropriate line using a bone folder or a strip of plastic that has been shaped to a rounded end. When a level of proficiency is reached in this method, the folder should be replaced with a craft knife and a cut made half-way through the card leaving, when folded, a very neat edge.

Figs. 6.19 and 6.20 show a model of a house made from balsa wood, sheet plastic, cardboard and plaster of Paris. The model is completed with modellers' surface finishes. Before constructing the model, the 15-year-old pupil selected his site and designed the house to fit in with its surroundings. The final result represents one term's work, from the first design to the completed model.

Fig. 6.19

Fig. 6.20

Figs. 6.21–3 show pupils at different stages of planning, building and finishing a model of a vehicle made from a truncated hexagonal prism.

In Fig. 6.21, students are studying commercial sales literature before starting the commercial livery design project (p. 145, q.2).

Fig. 6.21

Fig. 6.22 shows a student cutting out components ready for assembly.

Fig. 6.22

In Fig. 6.23, the model is being finished. Good graphic skills are essential, along with a knowledge of how to select equipment from the range available.

Fig. 6.23

EXERCISES

1. *Fig. 6.24 shows two views in first angle projection of a truncated hexagonal prism. They represent the cab section of a model lorry.*

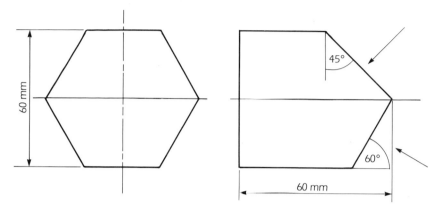

Fig. 6.24

Draw full size in first angle projection:
a) *the two views given;*
b) *an end elevation looking from the right of the front elevation;*
c) *the true shape of the faces indicated by the arrows on the front elevation; and*
d) *a development of the truncated hexagonal prism.*

On your development draw the windows, doors, etc., and add on 3–6 mm glue tabs on the appropriate sides. Fold the development carefully and glue.

Design your own back to the cab unit. You might wish to construct an articulated lorry, a flat-bed lorry, or a lorry and trailer.

Make a development drawing of your design, but remember that it must be to the same scale as your cab unit. Consider what type of product your vehicle is going to carry and draw on to your vehicle the appropriate Health and Safety signs. These signs are shown on p. 128. Finally cut it out and glue it together.

Wheels for your lorry can be easily made from dowel and the axles from welding rod. Further development drawings can be made for bumpers, mudguards and petrol tanks.

2. *You have been requested to design a company logo for use on all a company's correspondence, packaging etc., and also the livery suitable for use on commercial vans. Examples of the kind of vans the company might use are shown in Fig. 6.25 (overleaf). You should:*
i) *consider the type of commercial vans readily available and their relative size; and*
ii) *decide the name and product or service allied to the company and the type of goods that the van will be transporting.*

The company has two depots, one in Ashford, Kent and the second in Newcastle-upon-Tyne.
a) *Develop two logo designs. Select the better design and produce it to master quality.*
b) *Make a written statement as to why your final design is particularly suited to your selected company.*
c) *Select the type of van that you are going to use for your project.*
d) *Produce two alternative designs of the livery that is to be painted on to the vehicle. The designs must include the company logo and the vehicle's base town.*

e) Select your ultimate design and draw in pictorial projection a view of the van showing its full livery.

f) The company has now contracted you to make a flat one-piece development of your selected van that when unfolded will fit into an A4 size envelope. The model is to be erected by folding along indicated lines and secured by glue tabs.

g) The envelope is to have the company logo placed in the top left-hand corner.

h) Set up a display to include all your research material leading through to the final product.

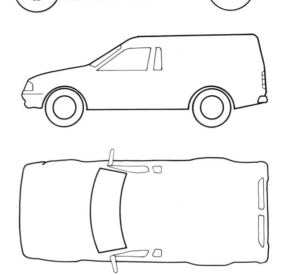

3. Fig. 6.26 shows three views in first angle projection of a landing craft suitable for transporting vehicles from a loading ramp to the beach.

a) Draw full size the development of the landing craft. Your landing craft must have loading and unloading facilities.

b) Design a suitable control cabin and make a development drawing.

c) Assemble your model. Consider the use of coloured card in its construction.

d) Indicate the Plimsoll line.

e) Research into the history of the Plimsoll Line as used on seagoing vessels, and present your research documentation with your model.

Fig. 6.25

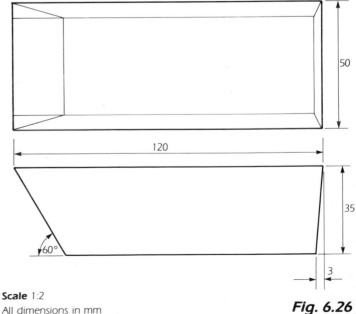

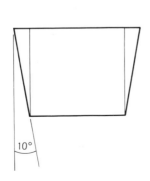

50

120

35

60°

3

10°

Scale 1:2
All dimensions in mm

Fig. 6.26

Index

The drawing has been completed.